# Classic Restaurants
## of
# ALEXANDRIA

# Classic Restaurants

## of

# ALEXANDRIA

HOPE NELSON

AMERICAN PALATE

Published by American Palate
A Division of The History Press
Charleston, SC
www.historypress.com

*Front cover, top left*: Hope Nelson; *top center*: Alexandria Library Local History Special Collections; *top right*: Hope Nelson; *bottom*: Alexandria Library Local History Special Collections.
*Back cover*: Alexandria Library Local History Special Collections; *inset*: Hope Nelson.

First published 2019

Manufactured in the United States

ISBN 9781467141130

Library of Congress Control Number: 2019950039

*For my parents, Brenda and Gil Nelson, who gave me life and made it beautiful*

# Contents

# CONTENTS

# Acknowledgements

I f there's one thing I've learned during this project, it's that it takes a village to write a book, and I've certainly been blessed with a supportive community that knows no bounds. There's no way I'll be able to adequately express my thanks, but I would like to try.

Kate Jenkins at The History Press has been a dream to work with. Kate comes armed with an abundance of patience that also doesn't preclude her from giving a swift kick in the pants when one is required. I don't know where this project would be without her ideas and guidance, but I can safely say this book wouldn't be in your hands without her.

The Local History and Special Collections department of the Alexandria Library has been invaluable in my research. Each librarian who calls Special Collections home is a wealth of knowledge and information that the city should be proud to have under its umbrella. Local History and Special Collections is such an incredibly valuable resource for all Alexandrians, and I encourage anyone interested in any remotely local topic to drop in and chat with a librarian. To a person, they have been so helpful and so supportive of this project, and it's meant the world to me.

Steven Mauren and Mary Kimm at the *Alexandria Gazette Packet* have been instrumental in helping me broaden my knowledge of the city's restaurant scene by providing me with a platform to keep Alexandrians up to date on all the latest dining news—and how it builds on the city's history. Plus, with their editing of every single article, they make me look better than I should. I'm truly appreciative.

Any time there's writing involved, I have Faye Milner to thank. My high-school journalism adviser and lifelong friend, she has helped me cultivate my prose from the earliest days and made me a better writer. Any success I have with the written word can be attributed in large part to her guidance, patience and focus. I treasure both her teachings and our friendship.

I thank my cousins, Gary Lewis and Michael Nelson, for being the best almost-siblings a kid could ask for. Gary, you have shown me what grace under pressure really looks like (and how to get the very highest level of tickets from a Skee-Ball machine). Michael, you've shown me how humor can save the day (or at least make it a lot more fun). I love you both.

My parents, Brenda and Gil Nelson, have been a constant cheering section for decades. You two have encouraged me every step of the way for the entirety of my life, and I can't begin to repay you. Your love and support have meant the world to me, and it's an honor to claim you both as mine. I adore you.

And finally, to Michael Pope, my husband and partner in crime (and in food). Part cheering section and part assignment editor, he has helped me carry this manuscript to the finish line, even when I wasn't sure we would make it there. I love you, LeeLee.

# Introduction

W alk down the streets of Old Town or Del Ray, or drive past the more suburban storefronts spread farther out within the city, and one thing is clear: There's no shortage of restaurants in Alexandria. From the casual to the high-end, the avant-garde to the down-home, there's a menu for nearly every palate and a cuisine for every tongue.

The restaurant business is a tough one. The common thinking is that at least 50 percent of restaurants fail within their first three years, and some estimates are higher still. Opening an eatery—and keeping it open—is an uphill battle that has to be fueled by passion for the food and a desire to serve the public. Otherwise, what's the use in trying?

Alexandria is an old city. Teeming with history, tracing its roots well before George Washington's era, the town is a microcosm of cultures, religions, socioeconomic statuses and more. Which is why it's no surprise, then, that its food culture is so diverse—and always has been.

And like the city itself, many restaurants have stuck around, weaving themselves into the fabric of the community over decades of service. Some launched at the dawn of the twentieth century and are still going strong, moving with the times and going online while still churning out cake after cake for satisfied customers. Some hosted birthnight and inaugural balls for the nation's founding fathers—and still manage to wake up for Sunday brunch. And some have remained a faithful place for neighbors to gather over a cup of coffee and a plate of bacon and eggs to chat over the events of the day.

The expanse of King Street has played host to a great many restaurants, past and present, over the years, making it an incredibly satisfying walk for residents and visitors alike. *Hope Nelson*.

But some eateries have shut their doors after years of service. Some fell prey to market conditions. Some cuisines fell out of favor with the changing trends and times. And for some, well, the owners just wanted to retire after a job well done. Though these establishments no longer grace the streets of Alexandria, their footprints still spark memories of meaningful times spent at the table, sharing a bite to eat.

Through this book, you'll come across old and new friends from a diverse range of cuisines. Start with a walk through history, from Washington's era right on through the twenty-first century, and explore an old—some say haunted—tavern that hosted both boarders and diners early on; a bakery whose jelly cakes have become part of Alexandria entertainment culture; an Italian landmark at the foot of King Street where power players have gathered nightly to enjoy a martini and maybe a cigar; and a restaurant that wouldn't be defined by urban renewal but rather moved with the times, down the street and around the corner.

Or take the spouse and children out for a family-friendly meal by feasting on the likes of a popular waterfront tavern known just as well for its weekend brunch as its lively happy hour. Or a go-to chili kitchen that spoons up four varieties of the spicy grub any number of ways. Harken back to the days of a pink-hued pizzeria sitting alongside Duke Street, known for its playful décor just as much as the hearty pizza that came out of the ovens. And don't forget to stop off for ice cream—at either of two across-the-street options.

Or maybe seafood is more your speed. Reminisce about the decades-old "inn" that sat proudly on the corner of King and Union Streets, just feet from the water. Or think back to a restaurant that sat *above* the water, atop pilings over the Potomac, where you could watch ships and sailboats glide past. Or venture a little farther afield and speed down the George Washington Memorial Parkway, arriving at a parcel of Washington's former land, for a taste of something comfortable but refined.

The diversity of international cuisine that Alexandria plays host to is also a sight—and taste—to behold. One of the region's very best Indian restaurants is in a subdued location in a strip-mall basement, but it never has trouble filling its dining room. Or venture to Baja California without even leaving the city limits with a Del Ray gem that has a line an hour long on the weekends. Think back to a grand French restaurant whose gargoyles kept watch over King Street for decades on end.

And, finally, fondly reminisce on those memorable renegades that have given the city its best stories over the years. The chatty Irishman who served presidents and pubgoers with the same warm welcome. The grocery store that brought organic specialty items to the streets of Old Town for the first time, well before a big-box store ever dreamed of doing so. Or the market in the public square that's been an Alexandria fixture for three centuries.

You'll remember many of these names right away: the Seaport Inn, Gadsby's Tavern, Chadwick's, Dishes of India, Beachcombers. For some, you may have to work a little harder to recall. (Where did you go after football practice at TC Williams was finished? Oh, yes. Burger Chef.) But each of these restaurants has demonstrated incredible staying power in an industry that doesn't always reward such stick-to-itiveness. They would have already earned a spot in Alexandria collective memory by purely existing for as long as they have—but their food, drink and ambiance make the picture complete.

So, put on your walking shoes and let's go on a tour of Alexandria's classic restaurants, past and present. You're guaranteed to learn a thing or two and maybe spark a new memory you hadn't thought about in thirty years. Come hungry. We've got a big meal in front of us.

# One
## From Washington to the Twenty-First Century

The tales of Alexandria's origins are as numerous as there are storytellers. From an old tavern's birth in the late 1700s to the mid-1800s arrival of what would become Alexandria's top-notch bakery, from two brothers launching an Italian restaurant on King Street that became the go-to place to see and be seen to a little pub a dozen blocks away that played host to bluegrass every night—the city's growth can be charted almost directly alongside its culinary history.

George Washington danced in the ballroom at one of the restaurants still open today. Another home-style eatery remains open after more than one hundred years of service and several residence changes. And a bakery closed its doors after a century, only to open again several years later online, paying homage to the past while preparing for the future in a twenty-first-century way. When it comes to Alexandria's history, the story is only just beginning, and its restaurant scene is telling the tale.

## GADSBY'S TAVERN, 138 NORTH ROYAL STREET

No chronicle of Alexandria's dining scene would be complete without Gadsby's Tavern. One of the few restaurants in Alexandria that can well and truly boast George Washington's presence on more than one occasion (to say nothing of President Thomas Jefferson several years later), Gadsby's

Tavern has seen more revolutions around the sun that any other Old Town restaurant still in service. From first presidents to modern-day tourists, the eatery and ballroom have seen traditions change while still holding on to long-ago favorite cuisines.

Opened in 1792 by Charles and Ann Mason, the tavern served for many years as the City Hotel, a rooming house for men (and the occasional Female Stranger). By the turn of the century—that is, the nineteenth century—it had become a restaurant and ballroom as well, hosting the likes of President Washington's "birthnight ball" in 1793 and 1799 and Thomas Jefferson's 1805 inaugural ball.

> *Fifteen rounds of cannon fire from the twelve pounders ushered in the day and continued to sound at intervals. After the President and leading men of the town had worshipped at Christ Episcopal Church, they assembled at Wise's for dinner at three o'clock. The gathering in the ballroom that day is typical of the banquets held in the two tavern buildings, for the company sat down to a table laden with the finest foods in season, all in great quantities, and then somehow the diners were equal to the fifteen toasts offered to everything and anything of patriotic or civic interest.*[1]

While the fanfare was certainly something to see, the décor itself was also a sight to behold.

> *The interior was done in such refined taste that no less than six United States presidents have used it for receptions and grand balls. The Blue Ballroom seemed quite small to me, especially when you think that such political notables as George Washington, Marquis de Lafayette, John Paul Jones, John Adams, Thomas Jefferson and James Madison were either doing the minuet or a little "do-si-doing" around this floor during one administration or another.*[2]

After the tavern site was purchased by the American Legion in the 1930s and then again by the City of Alexandria in 1972, it underwent extensive renovations to nearly every part of the building. On the eve of the bicentennial, it was ready to open to the public once more, with the hopes that President Gerald Ford might be a guest on the tavern's inaugural tour.[3]

> *"The tavern, famous for its use as George Washington's military headquarters and the site of first talks about a national constitution,*

Now, Gadsby's Tavern plays host to both a working tavern as well as a museum chronicling the history of the building and its occupants. *Hope Nelson.*

A military review takes place outside of Gadsby's Tavern in honor of the nation's bicentennial in 1976. *Alexandria Library Local History Special Collections.*

*will seat a total of 90 people in the restaurant and cocktail lounge areas. The menu is scheduled to include peanut soup, crab, roast beef, duck and a general seafood entry,"* added [City General Services Director Paul] *Schott.*[4]

The buzz surrounding the tavern restaurant—its opening signified by the bunch of grapes on the sign out front—brought awe from the public when its doors opened again in February 1976.

*In the restaurant, candle-like light glows on walls and tables. Dark wood reproduction Hepplewhite chairs and clothless tables are graceful in the dining rooms. There are oriental-style rugs and logs in the fireplaces (although these originally burned coal). Table service has the glint of pewter. The tap room just inside the front door is more casual, with bare floors and wooden coat pegs lining the walls. Costumed serving staff is everywhere, most attentive and apparently enjoying their novel surroundings.*[5]

Every year, Gadsby's Tavern hosts reenactment inaugural and birthnight balls in honor of the Founding Fathers. *Hope Nelson.*

In more modern times, the banquets and balls have largely given way to brunches, lunches and dinners for regular-Joe diners. But while the clientele has changed over the years, the ambiance remains very similar to what Washington and his ilk would have recognized.

> *Inside the restored 1792 hotel, it's Williamsburg without the three-hour drive. Chippendale chairs, dark bare wood tables, antique carved buffets and pewter place settings all gleam in the candlelight. The waiters are clad in breeches and buckled slippers, with lace jabots at their throats; the serving wenches wear full-hipped long skirts, laced bodices and bonnets.*[6]

Forget twenty-first-century staples like sushi and cronuts. Gadsby's menu hews closely to its roots: From a cup of peanut soup to Gentleman's Pye (lamb and beef in a red-wine sauce topped with mashed potatoes and served in a pie crust) to, of course, "George Washington's Favorite" (duck breast with rhotekraut and Washington's beloved corn pudding), the tavern has stuck with its niche to create a wonderfully historic-yet-modern experience for diners young and old.

# SHUMAN'S BAKERY, 516 KING STREET AND 430 SOUTH WASHINGTON STREET, NOW ONLINE

Long before mass-produced cookies and Christmas confections, there was one holiday tradition that rung in the season for generations of Alexandrians: Shuman's jelly cake.

A longtime bastion of Alexandria baking history, Shuman's has enjoyed a two-pronged life: first as a full-scale bakery; and now, in a new generation, a purveyor of its top seller and storied delicacy, the jelly cake.

Don't get the jelly cake confused with its siblings, the jelly roll or the jelly doughnut; it is neither. Rather, the light and airy dessert is a sheet cake of sorts, a kind of cake-turned-sandwich with layers of jelly nestled between the rows of cake and a dusting of powdered sugar topping it all off.

But to get to how the jelly cake came into being, it's better to go back to the beginning, when Shuman's was just getting started, back before it had developed the devotion of generations of Alexandrians.

Launched in 1876 by Louis Philip Shuman, the bakery became a mainstay in Alexandria. First on Fairfax Street and then at 430 King Street before settling for many years at 516 King, Shuman's Bakery served as both the livelihood and the residence for the Shuman family— Louis, his wife and their children lived above the shop[7]—and as sweet sustenance for the whole of the city. While the jelly cake quickly carved out its own place within the dessert hall of fame, it was by no means the only treat offered at Shuman's in those days. Indeed, the bakery was more of a tearoom in practice; cookies, pastries, cakes and, of course, bread all took top billing.

On almost an equal footing to the baked goods was the conversation. For decades, "The Bull Table" took up residence within the confines of the restaurant, turning the homey bakery into a modern-day salon.

*"It's the San Souci of Alexandria," said one longtime regular at the traditional early morning political pow-wow that transforms the sedate Shuman's Bakery into a rowdy, smoke-filled, backslapping bull session straight from "The Last Hurrah."*

*"They used to call it Shuman's Town Council," said 74-year-old city councilman Nick Colasanto, who says he has supped [sic] from Shuman's coffee cup every morning for the past 35 years.*

*"We'd all sit together at one long table in the back—the Bull Table. Politicians, businessmen, real estate people. We would discuss the*

*Right*: Shuman's Bakery, shown here in 1970, was a longtime mainstay in Old Town. *Alexandria Library Local History Special Collections.*

*Below*: Part bakery and part tearoom, Shuman's entertained Alexandrians for a century. *Alexandria Library Local History Special Collections.*

Sweets and treats line the walls in this 1903 view of Shuman's bakery. *Alexandria Library Local History Special Collections.*

> *issues of the day. As a joke, we asked the city to declare Shuman's a historical monument."*[8]

Writes Patricia Sullivan of the *Washington Post*: "The bakery was where residents came after church, and where bull sessions, dominated by good ol' boys proud of their 'Neanderthal conservatism,' as their prevailing political persuasion was termed at the time, ruled the early mornings, solving the world's problems (if only the world would listen)."[9]

Even the likes of the Queen of England couldn't resist a taste.

> *Jelly cake from Shuman's Bakery is an item so renowned that even Queen Elizabeth II has sampled it. As the Queen (then Princess) and Prince Philip were preparing to return to England in 1951, an order for hard rolls and jelly cake was placed with Shuman's for the royal couple to take with them. Many Alexandrians will agree that Shuman's is worthy of its international fame.*[10]

Indeed, it was the jelly cake that endured. After the fourth generation of Shumans, Lonny and Teddy Marchant, retired in 2004, the grand bakery closed its doors, seemingly for good. However, another half-dozen years hence found a renaissance of sorts: Another generation of Shumans made

Shuman's famous jelly cake is a staple of the holiday season—or any other special occasion. *Hope Nelson.*

the decision to resurrect the famous jelly cake, enthralling older and younger generations alike.

"It's part of my family's Alexandria tradition for years," Charlie Hulfish said. "I can remember as a kid being over at my grandparents' for Thanksgiving or Easter, the jelly cake there on the side table, and you'd just grab one, oh my."[11]

Shuman "youngsters" Patrick Hagan, John Leary and Marshall Shuman Hagan decided, as 2009 ticked away, to resurrect the famous jelly cake, using the family recipe to bring it back to holiday and celebratory tables citywide. "We started a Facebook page, and before you knew it, we had 100 or more Facebook fans, so we thought we'd look into it a little more in terms of restarting it as a family business," Hagan said. "We started up in November 2010. There was immediate response, and it's grown every year since."[12]

Today, Shuman's jelly cakes ship worldwide, and while the bakery's orders tick dramatically upward, the cakes are available year-round.

# PORTNER'S, NORTH ST. ASAPH STREET AND 5770 DOW AVENUE

Generally, once a longtime restaurant closes its doors, it remains in the historical and cultural memory only. But sometimes, it re-emerges no fewer than one hundred years later with the same name and the same family, albeit in a new location. Such was the case with Portner's, a longtime Alexandria staple in the 1860s that saw a resurrection in 2017.

Family patriarch Robert Portner immigrated to Alexandria from Prussia in 1853 and within a decade had set up shop with partner Frederick Recker to create Portner and Recker's Grocery Store in 1861. As the Civil War began and Union troops began to flood Alexandria, Portner watched the need for alcoholic beverages rise—and jumped onto the scene. He and three other business partners began to brew small batches of beer, selling them to the thirsty troops and other residents of the city. Near the end of the war, he sold off his investment of the grocery shop and opened the Robert Portner Brewing Company—which operated what was known as the Tivoli Brewery—in 1865.[13]

The brewery set up shop at the intersection of St. Asaph and Pendleton Streets in Old Town Alexandria, carving out a niche for itself and answering the city's call for beer. Despite a rocky start during Reconstruction, the business began to thrive, and Portner remained at the helm until his death in 1906.[14]

"It became the largest brewery in the southeastern United States, with distribution from Alexandria to Florida," Portner's great-great-granddaughter Catherine Portner said in an interview with the *Alexandria Gazette Packet* in 2017.[15] The brewery continued apace after Portner's death under the leadership of his sons until Prohibition forced the business's closure in 1916.[16]

The Tivoli Brewery, shown here in 1916, was Robert Portner's brainchild and continued to prosper until a decade after his death in 1906. *Courtesy of the Portner family.*

By all accounts, that was the grand finale for Portner Brewing Company. The site moved on to other enterprises, and the beer stopped flowing. Even after Prohibition was a thing of the past, the Portners themselves had found other ventures to occupy their time. And that was where the story was poised to end—until two of Portner's great-great-granddaughters, Margaret and Catherine Portner, concocted a plan to resurrect the brewery 101 years later.

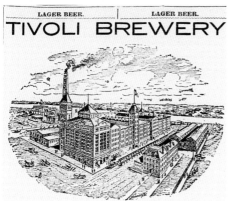

*Above*: The original site of Portner Brewery, shown here in 1882, launched several generations' worth of the business. *Courtesy of the Portner family.*

*Left*: The Tivoli Brewery, illustrated here in 1897, got its name by spelling "I Lov It" backward. Two of its best-selling lagers were Tivoli Hofbrau and Tivoli Cabinet. *Courtesy of the Portner family.*

> *Portner's…hews to its historical roots while also balancing some new directions. The brewhouse will sport three beer series—a Pre-Prohibition series, brewmaster seasonals, and, soon, offerings from its craft-beer test kitchen, which is a development program for home brewers who may one day wish to become brewmasters at their own production facility.*[17]

Situated in Alexandria's West End, Portner Brewhouse offered a wide array of German and American fare to go along with its brews. And the brews themselves were just a stone's throw away from guests; the brewery itself stood just behind the bar, a showpiece and focal point for the restaurant.

The renewed Portner Brewhouse served guests on the West End for a year before closing its doors in 2018, a victim of rising rents. But the family name remains strong in Alexandria, and its beers won't be forgotten.

## ROYAL RESTAURANT, 109 NORTH ROYAL STREET AND 730 NORTH ST. ASAPH STREET

Look around town for the oldest continuously operated restaurants, and the Royal Restaurant jumps up toward the very top of the list. Opening its doors in 1904 at 109 Royal Street, the Royal has seen Alexandria grow up around it—and has seen itself grow and change over the years, too, including adopting a new address (that isn't even on North Royal Street).

> *A century ago, the Royal Cafe, as it was called then, was in the heart of Old Town, at 109 Royal St., right next to City Hall.* [Current owner Charlie] *Euripides's uncle bought the restaurant in the 1930s, and it has been in the family ever since. It was, as a blurb on the menu describes it, the place where "local politicians, attorneys, businessmen and downtown citizens discussed the hot topics of the day over hearty southern-style dinners and rice pudding desserts."*
>
> *But during the Depression, Euripides said, it was also a place where, according to his uncle, ordinary people would come in search of work or a meal, offering to scrub floors in exchange for a bowl of soup.*[18]

Over time, the Royal became a hallmark of Alexandria, a stalwart in the food landscape of the city. It doesn't claim to be the hippest, hottest, trendiest spot—instead, it offers up a more family-friendly appeal, drawing both parents with children as well as businesspeople, working and retired, in for breakfast, lunch or dinner.

The Royal Café remained on Royal Street, in the shadow of City Hall, until the city's "urban renewal" project hit its stride in the 1960s. During the urban renewal phase of Alexandria city government, dozens of Old Town buildings were torn down in the name of progress; the Royal Café fell prey to the same fate in 1964. Shortly after the original café was torn down, the Royal Restaurant opened in a new location at 730 North St. Asaph Street.

> *"The city would not even let us take the restaurant equipment out of the building before bulldozing it," Euripides sadly recalled. "I still remember seeing my uncle standing across the street with tears streaming down his face as he watched the building come down."*
>
> *According to the restaurant's website, Euripides and his uncle were "undaunted by the uncompensated taking of their prime location" and in 1965 moved "The Royal" to its present location on North St. Asaph*

*Street. Euripides, by now married and raising a family, was determined that the new Royal Restaurant would be a success.*

*"This was our only income," Euripides said. "I couldn't let my uncle or my employees down."[19]*

It wasn't long before the new St. Asaph location became a settled home for the Royal Restaurant. And with it came fans and friends young and old who made the venerable old establishment part of their routine, settling into the well-worn booths with a view of the street. The most faithful of regulars don't even have to give the waitstaff their orders when they sit down; soon, out comes their normal fare, as though they'd called ahead.

*Euripides knows that it is such personal touches along with the restaurant's reliable presence that inspires loyalty in his customers, in spite of the restaurant's utter lack of trendiness and a decor that features dropped ceilings, red vinyl-upholstered booths and navy-and-white vinyl-checked tablecloths.*

*"We are a very traditional restaurant," says Euripides, a soft-spoken 70-year-old with a ring of white hair and bespectacled, soulful brown*

The Royal Restaurant, an Old Town favorite since 1904, has called several addresses home over the years but now resides on St. Asaph Street, several blocks (and streets) away from its original location. *Hope Nelson.*

More than a century on, the Royal Restaurant remains a gathering place for locals to chat over the events of the day and enjoy home-style fare. *Hope Nelson.*

The Royal Café remained on Royal Street, in the shadow of City Hall, until the city's "urban renewal" project hit its stride in the 1960s. *Hope Nelson.*

*eyes. "The heart and soul of this restaurant has always been the idea that the family was involved, at the door shaking your hand when you come in, greeting guests just like you do when they come to your house."*[20]

And for 115 years, the Royal has been the heart and soul of Old Town—a cozy, comfortable slice of home.

## MOUNT VERNON INN, 3200 MOUNT VERNON MEMORIAL HIGHWAY

It's a rare restaurant that gets the opportunity to sit in the cradle of American history, but the Mount Vernon Inn is afforded just that chance. For the better part of a century, the restaurant has offered a front seat to local visitors and tourists from all corners of the globe, ensuring that diners are fed not just a quick bite of "museum food" but higher-quality, more memorable fare.

Initially operated as a private concession, in 1981, the Inn was sold to the Mount Vernon Ladies Association, which also owns George Washington's mansion itself. It's been operating with the association ever since and, like the mansion, continues to draw in a crowd year after year.

Like Gadsby's Tavern, the modern-day Inn aims to get into the spirit of colonial times with a historical menu, eighteenth-century décor and waitstaff in period dress.

In 1974, *Washington Post* food writer Donald Dresden wrote:

> *The Mount Vernon Inn, just outside the gate to the historic estate, is a pleasing establishment that attempts to evoke the memory of colonial days with its décor, food, menu prose and servitors in early American dress....*
>
> *The menu includes four salads (95 cents to $2.75); seven sandwiches ($1 to $2.45); nine entrees of meat, fish and fowl ($2.50 to $3.75); soups (60 cents a cup, 90 cents a bowl); and desserts about 60 cents.*[21]

Since 1973, locals and visitors alike have been able to access the historic property via the Mount Vernon Trail, a bicycle and pedestrian path that spans eighteen miles and terminates at Mount Vernon. The two-wheeled trip to the historic site ends with quite a heart-pumping hill for the last mile or so, ensuring that diners have worked up an appetite by the time they arrive on premises.

Now run by the Mount Vernon Ladies Association, the Mount Vernon Inn has been feeding tourists and locals for decades. *Hope Nelson.*

Over the years, the Mount Vernon Inn enjoyed the occasional facelift, though the menu has remained comfortingly similar from season to season and decade to decade. *Hope Nelson.*

It didn't take long for cyclists—and foodies—to explore all that the Mount Vernon Inn had to offer at the end of their rides. In 1977, *Post* reporter Paul Hodge gave an extensive review of the Inn's best and brightest—by bike.

> *The tavern, which offers meals and sandwiches with colonial names and moderate prices, has become a haven for many of the 200,000 bicyclists a year who now pedal the route George Washington followed on horseback and carriage between his country estate, town house in Alexandria and the nation's new capital at the time (Philadelphia).*
>
> *Called the Little Hatchet Tavern when it opened in 1931, the inn offers a waffle and eggs breakfast at its snack bar ($2) beginning at 9 a.m. daily when Mount Vernon's gates open. On weekends, which is rush hour on the bike trail, an early morning snack bar meal may be the most peaceful....*
>
> *Now the inn opens for the day for brunches and lunches at 11 a.m. Its dark, cool dining rooms, with fresh flowers on the tables and waitresses swirling about in calico dresses and Martha Washington bonnets, are a welcome sight to warm and weary cyclists.*[22]

Peanut and chestnut soup, roast duck and crab cakes all take top billing at the Mount Vernon Inn, and the bread remains fresh and flavorful from visit to visit. *Hope Nelson.*

Over the years, the Mount Vernon Inn enjoyed the occasional facelift, though the menu has remained comfortingly similar from season to season and decade to decade. Peanut and chestnut soup, roast duck and crab cakes all take top billing, and the bread remains fresh and flavorful from visit to visit.

> *Good baking is clearly one of the kitchen's attributes, which it shows off first with its homemade breads and last with its homemade cobblers.... That bread basket is stocked with homemade crackers, large rounds that are rich enough to do without butter....Whole wheat bread, a dense yeasty bread with a crusty surface, is clearly the standout in this crowd.*[23]

While the menu has remained relatively similar over the years, the Inn has also kept with the times. Vegetarian and vegan offerings are now featured, as is the happy hour, perhaps in a different form than George Washington's social hours used to take. "Beer dinners," where local breweries pair their best beers with multicourse meals, are now consistently on the calendar from month to month, and brunches for every occasion—Mother's Day, Easter, you name it—are also by-reservation events.

By hewing to its history but also branching out as the decades roll on, the Mount Vernon Inn keeps turning out meal after meal from its kitchen, fusing the past with the present—and the future, too.

# LANDINI BROTHERS, 115 KING STREET

Stride along lower King Street and you'll soon come upon a tasteful, dignified storefront that gives way to a warm, historic dining room and bar. A spot both for those looking for a dressy, special night out and for the regulars who sidle up for their favorite drink each and every night, Landini Brothers is a longstanding hidden gem, a stalwart in a sea of the ever-changing business landscape.

Launched in 1979 by Franco and Noe Landini, it could be argued that Landini Brothers hasn't changed a great deal in the decades since. Its deep red hues, stone walls and wood-paneled bar harken back to another time, when dining out was the exception rather than the rule, when dinner was an event.

Several years after it opened, reviewers from the *Washington Post* dropped by to give it a go. "Stone walls, beam ceilings and crisp white tablecloths create an air of rustic country elegance. The diners might be wearing tuxedos or sport shirts. The maitre d' paces the slate floors with a smile. And everyone appears to be having a splendid time."[24]

Landini Brothers has been open now for forty years, but it hasn't aged a day. *Hope Nelson.*

And they are today as well, keeping the dining room comfortably full while feasting on Landini's pasta and other Tuscan favorites.

Keen watchers of Landini Brothers' foot traffic will notice a strange phenomenon as day turns to night: Some patrons will bypass the dining room and bar altogether, opting instead to jaunt upstairs to parts unknown, sometimes not to be seen again for several hours. The secret? Landini also plays host to CXIII Rex, a private cigar bar that opened in the shadow of Virginia's smoking ban, which forbids any lighting up in restaurants.

The loophole? With a separate ventilation system, old Rex is in the clear.

*The concept for CXIII Rex took form when the Landinis learned that Virginia would pass its own smoking ban in December 2009. Prior to that, a specific dining room in their restaurant allowed cigar smoking, but the younger Landini recognized that the room offered much more than an opportunity to smoke a cigar. It represented a lifestyle, and he wasn't about to let that disappear. "We were sitting on a golden opportunity to do something really great," he says. "We've never done anything half-assed before and we weren't about to start."*[25]

Restaurants for all palates dot the landscape in the 100 block of King Street. *Hope Nelson.*

With cigars upstairs and pasta downstairs, Landini Brothers has continued to find new ways to surprise and delight customers from all walks of life. The bastion of lower King Street has straddled two centuries; its life ahead seems to stretch as far as the longest strand of spaghetti, with plenty of spice to carry it through along the way.

## TIFFANY TAVERN, 1116 KING STREET

For decades, it wasn't unusual for pedestrians strolling along King Street to hear the strands of a banjo playing—maybe a mandolin, too—and listen to the dulcet sounds of a bluegrass band as they picked their way along to the delight of Tiffany Tavern's patrons. As the tavern was long considered the very best place in the D.C. area to hear a good bluegrass show, its life stretched for three decades, dawning in 1980 and staying vibrant until its final night in 2013.

> *That's the ongoing legacy of Theodore Karanikolas, known to all as Ted, who purchased the unpretentious little Old Town pub in 1980, changing its name from Mark Anthony to Tiffany Tavern on account of the lamp shades and stained glass within.*
>
> *"When I bought it, there was a trio playing at Mark Anthony's, a bluegrass sort of trio," says Karanikolas in the still-thick Greek accent of his youth on the Aegean island of Lesbos. "They were young, and I liked them very much and asked them to stay; and it all basically started from there."*[26]

Admittedly, the unassuming bar and grill wasn't much to look at to a casual passerby, but the heart of the place rested just inside the front door, where a small stage played host to band after band over the years, often with the members' backs pressed up to the window facing King Street. One step in told patrons all they needed to know—the audience raucous but polite, the bands lively and toe-tapping, the waitstaff busily working their way from table to table, barstool to barstool.

Bluegrass was the watchword of Tiffany Tavern from day one.

> *Bob Perilla, who performs regularly at Tiffany Tavern with his band, Big Hillbilly Bluegrass, says it's an honor to play there, because implicit in the*

Now, the former Tiffany Tavern location is a Mexican restaurant. *Hope Nelson*.

Tiffany Tavern, pictured here circa 1990, was the premier spot for bluegrass in Northern Virginia during its time. *Alexandria Library Local History Special Collections.*

Mexican restaurant Los Cuates has taken over the Tiffany Tavern location, though the tavern's exterior window design persists. *Hope Nelson.*

*booking is Karanikolas's seal of approval. "He's listened to two or three bluegrass bands a week, week in and week out for 21 years, so he really knows the music," Perilla says. "Occasionally a new band will be booked in there that's unaware that Ted is an expert, and they'll sometimes be very hurt when he tells them at the end of the night that they're not good enough to come back."*[27]

After thirty-three years, Tiffany Tavern closed its doors in spring 2013 when its owners decided to retire. The building now plays host to a Mexican restaurant—and the bar's window looking out onto the street remains intact.

## Two

# Family Dining from Age to Age

From down-home American fare to pizzerias, Alexandria's families have sat down at the tables of a plethora of cuisines over the years. The menus of the restaurants they visit may take many forms— hearty chili, juicy burgers, soft and cheesy pizza and, yes, the occasional beer or wine for Mom and Dad—but the characteristics of what makes a family-friendly establishment are largely similar from place to place.

Homey. Cozy. Welcoming to even the littlest, perhaps loudest guests while not forsaking the more sullen teenagers and also giving a knowing nod and supportive smile to the adults at the table. It takes a village to raise a family, sure, but it also takes a community to feed them, especially when they're out in the public square. Maybe they're touring, visiting a new town during cherry blossom season. Maybe their native Alexandrian roots run three generations deep. But regardless, these restaurants have hosted the very best in family dining, both past and present.

## CHADWICKS, 203 STRAND STREET

The high-water marks memorialized in brass plaques on the interior column belie Chadwicks' proximity to the Potomac River, and while the neighborhood grill has seen some adventures over time, its scars lend the restaurant character indeed. An Alexandria stalwart for forty years, Chadwicks' history

A 1978 view of the future site of Chadwicks, which opened its doors in 1979. *Alexandria Library Local History Special Collections.*

This alley, shown here in June 1978, is now enclosed within the Chadwicks restaurant. *Alexandria Library Local History Special Collections.*

is rooted in a culture that is at once a family-friendly dinner experience, a happy-hour hot spot and a place to kick back on Sundays and watch football games while bellying up to the bar.

The restaurant—the kid brother to the original Chadwicks in Georgetown, which opened in 1967—opened its doors in 1979, taking up residence in a long and storied location that had seen plenty of triumph and tragedy over the centuries. The footprint that Chadwicks sits on dates back to the mid-1800s, when the warehouses and wharves had been rebuilt from an 1811 fire. "An 1847 tax ledger lists a 'wharf and house on the alley and the Strand' with a value of $15,000. It is this structure which, incorporating perhaps some of the 1811 foundation, left parts of its grand stone and lower brick walls to Chadwicks."[28]

Much of the waterfront was again destroyed in 1897 in one of the worst fires in Alexandria history, but within a decade, DeWilton Aitcheson, who owned the now-burned property, had begun to build again, creating the façade that so many Alexandrians would now recognize as a favorite restaurant.

> *Building on the two-foot thick solid stone foundations and the standing bricks, Aitcheson erected the two-story structure we see today with its pitched roof and parapet. For the next quarter century, the warehouse served successively as an assembly shop (1907), a warehouse for the storage and tanning of hides (1912) and an electric light supply house (1921). During the depression years of the 1930s, it stood vacant. In 1941 it was reborn as a steam laundry.[29]*

In 1957, the building was once again threatened by fire but found itself just outside of the damage when all was said and done. By 1978, the building had been taken over by commercial real estate managers Strand Street Associates, and Georgetown Holdings—the managers of the original Georgetown Chadwicks as well as the operators of Gadsby's Tavern for the better part of a decade[30]—leased the space with the aim of opening a second Chadwicks there on the waterfront. "The Alexandria restaurant opened its doors to diners in early 1979 and, in 1985, added the atrium dining area in the narrow corridor through which horse-drawn carts once clattered, carrying goods to the commission houses and wharves."[31]

Throughout its lifetime, Chadwicks' modus operandi has been largely unchanged: The kitchen serves up good, down-home American-style food at a good price. From a passel of burger options (which have grown over

Through hurricanes and floods, Chadwicks has remained a stalwart of Alexandria dining. *Hope Nelson.*

time to include turkey and veggie patties) to crab cakes and to bar snacks such as nachos and fried green tomatoes, diners have had plentiful options that stand the test of time. And while occasionally new chefs have worked to put their own spin on the menu, at the end of the day the fare harkens back to where it started—pub food with a decidedly Alexandrian twist.

The worst-kept secret at Chadwicks is its robust (and affordable) weekend brunch. From classics such as omelets and French toast to Old Town favorites such as a "Scottish scramble" featuring smoked salmon and cream cheese served with an English muffin and home fries, the menu offers too many tempting choices—and affordable adult beverages, as well. Though the days of ninety-five-cent champagne glasses are long gone (but only by a decade as of this writing), mimosas still ring in at four dollars and a bottle of champagne will set you back fourteen dollars.

The down-home feel of the restaurant is what keeps it popular, wrote the *Alexandria Times* in 2017:

> *The restaurant's longevity is often attributed to its constant crowd of locals, many of whom have been coming to the restaurant for decades. Serving those long-time patrons is a staff that also has many multiyear veterans,*

*such as manager and longtime bartender Karen Bettius, who started at the restaurant in 1998.*

*"I just really liked the people here. The customers would say 'welcome to the bar,'" Bettius said. "We had two bartenders who worked here who had so much fun on Friday and Saturday nights. I don't think they even did it for the money—they were doing it for the fun of it. You could tell because they were in their glory. They were making people sing to the jukebox. It was fun."*[32]

For years, Chadwicks sported several siblings, including another longtime location in Washington, D.C.'s Georgetown neighborhood, but as management changed hands and the dining landscape morphed throughout the region, only the Alexandria location remains. The waterfront simply wouldn't be the same without its faithful overseer, home to many a brunch, lunch and dinner over decades of service.

## HARD TIMES CAFÉ, 1404 KING STREET

Alexandria's Old Town just wouldn't be the same without its favorite chili purveyor, Hard Times Café. A fixture in the community since 1980, Hard Times' history actually stretches back much further than that. Cooking chili was in the blood of the founding brothers, Jim and Fred Parker, and their occupational lineage stretches back to their grandfather, a Texan born in the 1870s who put down roots in Oklahoma.

The Parker brothers were turned on to Washington, D.C.'s Texas Chili Parlor in the 1960s; when it closed in 1971, Jim Parker began to host a "chili parlor" of sorts in his own home for family and friends. By 1980, the brothers had decided to make a professional run at a chili business—and Hard Times was born.

*In 1981, Fred Parker opened the first Hard Times restaurant in a two-story row house on King Street in Old Town Alexandria. Parker and his brother Jim renovated the building, laying the brick floor and hanging on the walls old photos taken by their father. Fred Parker modeled the restaurant after the former Old Texas Chili Parlor in the District, owned and operated by Hazel Calloway until her death in 1971. A year later, the brothers left their day jobs to work full time at Hard Times Café.*[33]

*Left*: The façade of Hard Times Café, shown here in 1990, has changed little in the ensuing decades. *Alexandria Library Local History Special Collections*.

*Below*: A pedestrian walking past Hard Times Café in 1984 would find King Street to be a different landscape than it is today. *Alexandria Library Local History Special Collections*.

The Hard Times Café on King Street is the original in the franchise, which has grown over time. The narrow storefront gives way to a two-story restaurant with plenty of seating despite first appearances. As country western music plays on the stereo system and throngs of patrons chow down on the likes of chili mac and cornbread, it's clear that this "chili parlor" hews closely to its Texas and midwestern roots—and one taste of the chili proves it's the real deal.

But in 1983, when the *Washington Post* reviewers came a-calling, King Street was still in the throes of a renewal process, changing its look from a more rough-edged veneer to a tourism hot spot.

> *The prices at this cheerful chili house partly reflect its location: a stretch of King Street that investors and urban redevelopers so far have ignored. It's a neighborhood in transition—at least poised for transition, which is bound to begin once the Metro opens two blocks away.*
>
> *There are art and antique galleries here and there, otherwise the area includes a used-car lot, a Laundromat, a wholesale restaurant supply house, shells of stores boarded up and drab houses with fake stone fronts. And there, like a buttercup blooming in the pavement, is the Hard Times Café.*[34]

Over the years, King Street grew in prominence and scale, and soon Hard Times was no longer the new kid on the block, the only dining spot for as far as the eye could see. But rather than grow into a flashy nouveau riche establishment, it stayed true to its roots.

> *There ought to be horses hitched up outside; they'd fit right in with the huge pots of chili steaming behind the bar, and with the walls sporting armadillos, a cowskin, real longhorns (which came from Texas on a first-class Concorde seat), barbed wire and photographs that the owners' father took when he was in Wyoming back in '22.*
>
> *Hard Times has one of the best country-and-western jukeboxes around—many foot-tapping customers would bet the ranch on it. One woman, digging for quarters in her skirt pocket, said she comes to Hard Times because of the jukebox; she doesn't even like chili.*[35]

The menu, too, keeps Hard Times' chili-parlor origins within close reach. Diners can choose from four different kinds of chili, including a vegetarian option. (Not sure what to pick? Your server will give you a taster

The red-brick façade of Hard Times Café belies the hues of chili served inside. *Hope Nelson.*

of each one to help you decide.) They then select how to have it served. The chili mac—chili atop a bed of spaghetti—is a perennial favorite, but other styles have entered the culinary lexicon in more recent times, including Frito chili pie (chili atop a pile of corn chips) and chili taters (chili atop Tater Tots). There's also a chili salad for the more, ahem, health-conscious among the clientele.

As time has gone by, the menu has begun to sport more non-chili offerings, as well, including an array of sandwiches and salads—but the jukebox music, western décor and down-home atmosphere always bring diners back to the hearty entrée at hand…with a slice of cornbread on the side.

## SOUTHSIDE 815, 815 SOUTH WASHINGTON STREET

It's easy not to consider Southside 815 a long-tenured restaurant. In fact, it's easier still to consider it an Alexandria staple, one that somehow defies the hands of time and both remains a comfortable old friend and adds spice to the menu every so often with new items. But though it may not seem so, Southside is a good quarter-century old, having come onto the scene in July 1993 and created an immediate following.

And that following is still in full force today. Pop into Southside on a sunny summer Saturday and you've got little hope of moseying straight over to one of the restaurant's outdoor tables without a bit of a wait. Come in on a dark January evening after a foot of snow has fallen on the ground and you'll find dozens of others lifting a glass and toasting Mother Nature. For football games and Stanley Cup finals, post-parade happy hours and regular Wednesday nights, Southside draws a crowd, both in the bar and in its dining room.

As its name evokes, Southside's bread and butter—or perhaps its cornbread and hot pepper jelly, as it were—is southern fare. And as *Washington Post* food critic Phyllis Richman raved not long after the restaurant's opening, the restaurant quickly became one of the best southern-food purveyors in the area:

> *A true Southern restaurant tempts you to fulfill the mainstay of our nutritional guidelines—five or more servings of fruit and vegetables a day—all at one sitting. Greens, succotash, sweet potatoes, mashed potatoes and fried green tomatoes: At Southside 815 I could happily skip the meat*

*and make a meal of the side dishes. Add corn, bread-and-butter pickles and a salad, and I'm halfway into tomorrow's requirements. The butter, the cream, the sugar, the cooking oil? Well, nobody's perfect.*

*The point is, this quiet, unassuming Alexandria restaurant comes as close as any of our new restaurants to being a real Southerner. The greens alone leave all local competitors in the dust.*[36]

At 815 South Washington Street, Southside 815 replaced former restaurant Que Sera and never looked back. Though, even today, diners will find some lingering hints of the restaurant's former identity lingering around. The booths that sit in little nooks? Those haven't changed from Southside's predecessor. But, by now, those remnants have become instead a part of the decades-old southern eatery, instead of harkening back to restaurants past.

Writes Richman: "Southside 815 is a most compelling place to settle in with a beer and a po' boy and hang out for the evening. And the prices are low enough that filling up the table with side dishes seems like a very sensible idea."[37]

Recently, Southside 815 became an older sibling to Northside 10, the restaurant on Glebe Road that replaced the multi-decade stalwart Chez Andrée. But success and age haven't seemed to dampen the original's enthusiasm for life and what all comes next.

## UNION STREET PUBLIC HOUSE, 121 SOUTH UNION STREET

Walk toward the Potomac River along King Street and hang a right when you get to the last street before the waterfront. There, half a block down, you won't possibly be able to miss the stately red-brick restaurant rising out of an eighteenth-century warehouse. The Union Street Public House, a mainstay in Old Town Alexandria since December 1986, has made itself right at home amid the historical surroundings—so much so that it looks much older and more historic than it has any right to be (in all good ways, of course).

The pub, which spans four lots along Union Street, has roots centuries deep—the building that now stands at 123 South Union has been in place since the 1790s. While fire destroyed the surrounding buildings over time, the renovated warehouse at 123 remains, its façade largely unchanged from its original years in service.

A hallmark of Old Town's Union Street, the Union Street Public House offers an expansive dining room and multiple bars. *Hope Nelson.*

*Right*: Since 1986, Union Street Public House has made its home in an eighteenth-century warehouse. *Hope Nelson.*

*Below*: The building that now stands at 123 South Union has been in place since the 1790s. *Hope Nelson.*

> *Old Town Alexandria has a new olde pub and everybody loves it. Singles love it, couples love it, moms and dads and kiddies love it. The bar is a crowd scene. The dining rooms always seem filled. I have never encountered—at least outside the Roy Rogers milieu—so high a proportion of parents-and-children in a single dining room on a Saturday night. And it is not just because Union Street serves the world's biggest Shirley Temples.*[38]

Of course, diners today are used to Union Street Public House fitting in quite well with its Old Town surroundings, nestled as it is between blocks of historic townhomes and storefronts. And while the building's outside has kept a well-aged veneer, the inside is as cozy and comfortable as any modern restaurant should be. Friday nights will find a bustling bar scene as Alexandrians knock off work and tourists pop in for a refreshment; Sunday mornings will find sleepy-eyed families and churchgoers alike bellying up to a table for the weekend brunch.

> *The food at Union Street, like the clientele, includes a little bit of everything. The accent is strongly American—hearty and inventive....The amazing thing is that while this menu sounds like jack-of-all-trades overreaching, it works. Faults are there to find, but the food tastes good, satisfies and leaves you undecided only about whether to order more of the same next time or to try something new.*[39]

Being just across the street from the river can put one in a seafood frame of mind, and the location affords Union Street Public House the opportunity to highlight some of the Mid-Atlantic's best, from cherrystone clams to Atlantic salmon. The business-lunch set will find steaks and pork chops more to their liking, and those looking for a beverage to wet their whistle will be pleased with the 1986 Whiskey Bar, a niche near the back of the restaurant dedicated to whiskey from around the region—and the world.

But through the array of dining rooms and bars, amid the throng of families and happy-hour-goers, Union Street has remained a representative of a true "public house" for more than three decades. While merging the old with the new, it has kept its identity fully intact, paying homage to the pubs of yore while also looking ahead to the century that stretches out ahead.

# GENEROUS GEORGE'S POSITIVE PIZZA & PASTA PLACE, 3006 DUKE STREET

Any Alexandrian living in the city during the last quarter of the twentieth century couldn't possibly miss Generous George's. Ensconced in a pink façade and sitting merrily alongside the major artery of Duke Street, the pizzeria and pasta purveyor was an Alexandria mainstay for three decades before its closure in 2009. Known for its reasonable prices and family-friendly atmosphere as much as it was for its electric exterior—for years adorned as well with two nutcrackers keeping sentry watch next to the front door—Generous George's was a popular hangout for generations of residents.

"Generous George is a high-volume, much-loved pizza fun house strewn with '50s kitsch where everything is turned into a pizza," wrote *Washington Post* food columnist Phyllis C. Richman in November 1996. "Even the pastas are served on a pizza crust. This restaurant knows what it's about, because the pizza crust is its strongest suit. It's puffy and crispy, yeasty and chewy, a dreamboat pizza crust."[40]

Owner George Mansy's history with the property that Generous George's sat on ran deep.

> *When George Mansy was growing up on Duke Street, it was a two-lane paved dirt and gravel road. He lived on the upper floor of a house that existed to the left of where Generous George's is now located (where the Shell Oil station now sits). His parents ran a grocery store on the lower level, Uncle Vick's Market. When the owners decided to convert the house back to residential space, the Mansys moved next door and ran their grocery store from the space that occupies the right-hand space of Generous George's (where the entrance and pizza-ordering counter are).[41]*

Over time, the Mansy family moved and opened a pizzeria in Springfield but retained ownership of the Duke Street property. Thus it came to be that in 1977, George Mansy opened on the site a pizzeria and sub shop that was originally called the Yellow Deli Belly Buster. It was Mansy's mentor, Nick Latsios of Il Porto Ristorante, who encouraged the restaurant's name change to what it eventually became beloved for. "George credits the name change to Nick, who came into the restaurant one day and said, 'George, this is the biggest pizza I have ever seen, you are so generous. You should rename it,'" noted a February 2002 article in the *Alexandria Gazette.*[42]

Its popularity endured as the kitchen slung up pie after pie teeming with the likes of pepperoni, salami, olives, mushrooms and more. In 1987, Mansy expanded Generous George's, taking over the adjacent building and launching the pasta wing of the operation.[43] Over the years, Mansy opened nearly a dozen additional locations but later shuttered them all except for the Duke Street original.

> *Having been in business for so long, George enjoys seeing customers who started coming in when they were children now coming back with their husbands and children. Many of his former employees also come back in with their families. When George's sister, Theresa Cook, worked there, many of the TC Williams students came in. "She was the strength of the dining room," said George.[44]*

Families were often attracted to the bright, festive colors—and the respect and fanfare given to the littlest members of the group.

> *Generous George's eclectic, kid-appealing décor features ceiling tiles splashed with colorful paint squiggles and hung with rocking toys, old-fashioned formica-topped tables and replica carousel animals upon which children can sit. The menu includes make-your-own pizzas, available Monday through Wednesday. Kids eat free on their parents' birthdays.[45]*

Generous George's closed in 2009, and though signage over the years has touted the arrival of a new pizzeria, the building has remained dormant in the years since, though plans for a new pizzeria by another owner have been in the works for years. Only recently did the pink façade, which stood as a testament to decades of family business—and family customers—finally change its stripes, a mark of the passage of time, the dawn of a new era.

## TABLE TALK, 1623 DUKE STREET

The drive down Duke Street on the outskirts of Old Town has changed over the years. Buildings have gotten taller, condominiums have popped up over swanky grocery stores, whole new neighborhoods have materialized out of seeming thin air. But nestled in the middle of it all, comfortably remaining a stalwart of the area no matter what is going on around it, is Table Talk, a down-home diner that has been a constant for residents and tourists alike for more than forty years.

Walk into the restaurant today and it's akin to what it was when it first opened in 1975. The wood-paneled bar sports homemade desserts under glass cloches, tempting customers who have moseyed up to pay their bill. The lighting fixtures and décor root the restaurant in history in all the best ways. And the tables lining the windows are still the most coveted, giving diners an eye on the world passing by outside.

Customers and servers alike are regulars, some taking their place in Table Talk for decades.

> *Gloria Connor, a waitress at Table Talk, refills a cup with decaf coffee. Two couples are meeting for breakfast, one from Arizona. "We lived down the block at Carlyle Towers and used to come here. Our son lives in Alexandria and when we came back to visit we wanted to come back here." Today she got eggs Benedict. "I wanted to splurge."*
>
> *Connor has been working at Table Talk for three and a half years where she came after working 24 years at a different restaurant. She says many of her customers followed her to Table Talk. She switches to a carafe of regular coffee and heads for the corner. A customer volunteers, "Wednesday is reunion day. Eight of us who knew each other meet every week for breakfast."[46]*

While Table Talk started its life in the mid-1970s and has indeed remained a constant, it has changed with the times as well. In the early 2000s, the fate of the business was called into question as development continued all around it, making the venerable restaurant a very valuable piece of real estate. But in 2015, local businessman Jeff Yates purchased the restaurant, both moving it into the next era of life and protecting it from redevelopment. It's easy to see the balance beam that Table Talk is perched atop, protecting its identity while embracing new ideas.

> *The Table Talk restaurant on Duke Street has a meatloaf dish that is their big seller, even though it's an old school dish that has been around since they opened in 1975. Enter the internet and a new generation, and Table Talk is on the fence in a way. The Yates family, who own Table Talk, know where the new age of commerce is headed, but then there's the meatloaf and a couple of other dishes that are staples with many customers.*
>
> *"We're trying to keep it at a happy medium," said Michelle Riggleman, the manager at Table Talk. "It's like coming home to Grandma's house,"*

*she said. Roasted turkey comes in a close second, and it's the pancakes that tops the list in the mornings.*[47]

Yates died in early 2018, and his fiancée, Connie Sofia, now owns Table Talk. She has joined the restaurant on the balance beam as well, protecting what is beloved about the diner while keeping it current.

*Facebook, Instagram and Snapchat are part of her plan. "Everyone who follows us can see other families that have stopped in to dine with us and they can comment on each other's pictures, it's just building bridges for Yates Table Talk," said Sofia. "We're expanding the lines of communication."*

*Although the Yates family owns Yates Corner, a gas station complex near Del Ray, and Yates Sunoco in Kingstowne, saving Table Talk was a mission of theirs. Jeff Yates "was a regular and did not want to see it be turned into a high rise or office building, so as of June 2015, Yates Table Talk is here to stay," said Sofia.*[48]

## BURGER CHEF, SEVERAL AREA LOCATIONS

When Alexandrians of the 1960s had a hankering for a burger, there was an easy place to turn: Burger Chef. The franchise chain, which had locations on Duke Street, Franconia Road, Glebe Road, Mount Vernon Avenue and Richmond Highway, gained a foothold in Alexandria in the late 1950s and held on for dear life for decades.

The drive-in hamburger-and-shake cafés cropped up throughout the country beginning in 1958 and were second only to McDonald's in their heyday.

"It was first to market what has since become a fast food staple: the burger-fries-and-drink combo meal, dubbed the 'Triple Threat' and sold for just 45 cents," wrote Eric Dodds in *Time*.[49] By the early 1970s, the chain had hit its apex with 1,200 locations before slowly winding down throughout several decades under the management of General Foods.

But well before Burger Chef was a household name nationwide, Robert Holtzman served as the regional franchise director for Burger Chef and opened the first area location in Del Ray on Mount Vernon Avenue in June 1959. "Holtzman claimed that the store sold 2,000 hamburgers a day its first month in operation, beating his expectations," *Washington Post* reporter Frank C. Porter wrote in July 1959.[50]

Shortly following the Del Ray location came several others, including the West Glebe Road outpost, also opened by Holtzman on April 28, 1960. Alexandrian Frank Callahan went on to become the franchise's longtime manager, retiring in 1977, two years before his death in 1979.[51]

Townhomes now sit atop the site of the 706 Mount Vernon Avenue location; a Pizza Hut has taken up residence at 1049 West Glebe Road. But Burger Chef lives on in the memory of longtime Alexandrians whose hankering for a burger and shake extends beyond the bounds of time, reaching back decades to the era of drive-ins and the newly minted fast-food business.

## POP'S AND THE CREAMERY, 109 AND 110 KING STREET

There's a bit of an ice-cream war—a cold war, one might say—in effect on lower King Street. Just a block from the Potomac River, diners will find two shops almost directly across the street from each other, each scooping up a dizzying array of frozen wares. Pop's takes the north side of the street; the Creamery, formerly known as Scoop Grill, takes the south. And don't think Alexandrians are impartial. No, they've chosen sides.

Everybody's got a favorite, it seems, and thank goodness for both institutions that the populace is large and the tourists are booming.

Pop's, named after Ray "Pop" Giovannoni, has been a mainstay on King Street since 1998. The company touts that the original Pop began his tenure in the ice-cream business in the 1940s, and the shop's décor harkens back to that era. Black-and-white checkered floors and a bright-red serving counter beckon dessert-goers, and the vast array of ice-cream flavors keeps them coming back.

Many of Pop's recipes came from Schneider's Bakery in Washington, D.C., the *Alexandria Gazette Packet* wrote in 2003.

> *The bakery was renowned for the ice cream it produced, held by some to be the best in the city. Eleanor Roosevelt served it to White House guests.*
>
> *Pop, father of the owner's late husband, wrote down the recipes and kept them for almost 60 years. Now the shop operates as an old-fashioned ice cream parlor, making all ice cream on the premises.*[52]

Pop's scoops out ice cream to the masses, no matter the weather. *Hope Nelson*.

Pop's—sandwiched between the Fish Market and Landini Brothers—is a great place to pick up dessert. *Hope Nelson*.

The Scoop Grill, pictured here in 1985, has churned out tasty ice cream for decades. *Alexandria Library Local History Special Collections.*

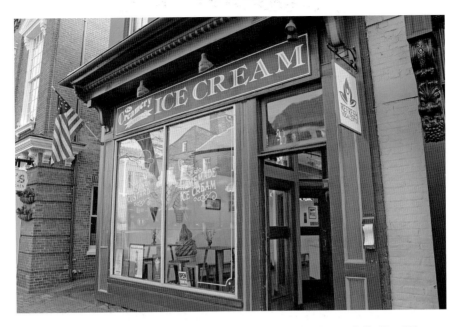

Now the Creamery, the ice cream parlor was formerly known as Scoop Grill. *Hope Nelson.*

The Creamery—known for most of its existence as Scoop Grill—touts itself as the city's oldest continually operating ice-cream parlor. The shop was founded in 1984 by Charlie and Lynne Lindsey and was purchased in 2018 by Edward Guerrero, continuing its reign without missing a beat.

"For more than 25 years, Old Town's oldest ice cream shop has won fans with its freshly spun ice creams and custards," writes Brianne Alcala in the *Washington Post,*[53] and she's not wrong. Like Pop's, its array of sweet treats is disorienting—but a perusal of the menu will help you find your way to a happy dessert in no time.

One thing is for certain: Both parlors have special flavors to explore.

Visitors could go the regular vanilla-and-chocolate route, sure, but why stick to standbys when s'mores, Bailey's mint chip and carrot cake are in the offing? Or why not go all-out and order up a sundae—both locations have their own specialties in that department—and chow down while perusing the waterfront just one block away?

As they battle for the block, the Creamery and Pop's both ensure that no matter what tickles your taste buds, there's always another flavor to try.

# JOE THEISMANN'S RESTAURANT, 1800A DIAGONAL ROAD

Longtime Washingtonians don't have to think long to remember Joe Theismann. Originally renowned for his time playing for the Washington Redskins, and then known almost as well for the gruesome injury that ended his career (editor's note: it's not advisable to replay footage of it), while still a football player Theismann went about rebranding himself in a most successful way: by becoming a restaurateur.

At one time, Theismann had six locations of his eponymous restaurant running concurrently, but over the course of three-plus decades, only one branch remains: the Alexandria location, situated neatly on the edge of Old Town and across the street from the King Street Metro station. Long after Theismann's injury and subsequent retirement in 1985, the restaurant that bears his name keeps chugging along, celebrating the victories and agonizing over the defeats of each of the sports teams that grace its bar-facing televisions every night.

Theismann entered the restaurant business while he was a pro football player barely reaching the prime of his career. In fact, many in Washington had not cottoned to him at all by the point when his would-be business partner, Vern Grandgeorge, first approached him about opening a restaurant.

*In 1975, Grandgeorge and his wife, Susan, had recently invested $5,000 in a restaurant concept that was searching for a celebrity athlete's brand recognition. The restaurant's other investors had originally wanted to name it Bill Toomey's, a track and field athlete who won the decathlon in 1968, but that idea fell through. The ownership also considered Jim "King" Corcoran, a quarterback who played for a number of different leagues from 1966 to 1975.*

*Attention eventually turned to Theismann, who was far from the team's most popular player at the time, having positioned himself against then-Redskins quarterback Sonny Jurgensen and second stringer Billy Kilmer. He famously posited to reporters that he wanted to start before both of them.*

*"I'll never forget sitting down with Vern....He said, 'Look, you came into town, you want the [quarterback] job, but people don't like you because what you said. Why would we put your name on a restaurant?'" Theismann recalled. "I said 'You have to look at it this way—things can only get better from here.'"[54]*

At one time, Joe Theismann had six locations of his eponymous restaurant running concurrently. But over the course of three-plus decades, only one branch remains: the Alexandria location on Diagonal Road. *Hope Nelson.*

The Alexandria outpost of Theismann's opened in 1986, and like the original location in Bailey's Crossroads, it immediately drew customers with its clear sports theme—first, of course, by the name of its owner, but then in all the touches that make a sports bar good. The televisions, the bar, the game-friendly snacks, the low-key but responsive nature of the waitstaff—all were in plentiful supply at Theismann's.

The same was true of Theismann's charm, on display as early as the mid-1970s, when—despite his comments provoking Washingtonians' ire early in his tenure with the Redskins—he began to carve out a niche for himself outside of football, exploring business opportunities in a wealth of industries, restaurants being only one of them. Wrote the *Washington Post* in 1980:

> *At age 30—he'll be 31 in nine days—Joe Theismann won't admit to having made his first million yet. But if he hasn't, he has at least almost that much in the bank. He is into oil wells, vitamins, precious metals, stocks, fast-food franchises, television movies and personal appearances. He earns with the help of bonuses, around $150,000 annually from the Redskins. His off-season income exceeds that figure and is growing every year.*

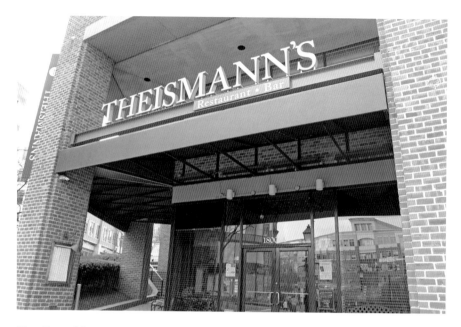

The Alexandria outpost of Theismann's restaurant opened in 1986 and is still going strong today. *Hope Nelson.*

> *Other than Sugar Ray Leonard, Theismann is the most popular and most visible athlete in Washington. He benefits handsomely by playing the key position on a team that is worshiped with cult-like allegiance by its fans. But he has not sat back and waited for the riches to pour in. He has gone out and grabbed them and reeled them in with the same kind of brash ambition he displays on the field.[55]*

With all of this in mind, it was really no wonder that his Old Town restaurant has stood the test of time. Its popularity spikes during years when the Redskins are in the hunt for a Super Bowl ring, but its success has remained stable from year to year, even in the case of a home-team slump.

In 2018, Theismann and Grandgeorge sold an equity share of the business to the Alexandria Restaurant Partners group, a partnership that holds a half-dozen other restaurants in its portfolio as well. The name remained, as did much of the management and staff, as well as the menu options.

Theismann told the *Alexandria Times* in 2018:

> *"What's neat about it is I can still see how it was when we started here 32 years ago. I can still walk in and see the pile of dirt where we were going*

to put the bar in the back room," Theismann said. "I can remember all the time we spent remodeling the place and the vision we had....At the time, we were one of only two retail establishments here. There were no hotels. There were no condominiums or a U.S. Patent Office or a federal courthouse."...

"Vern and I, we're not getting any younger and we want to be able to carry on the tradition. You want people to be able to continue to enjoy the experience," Theismann said.[56]

# THE DAIRY GODMOTHER (FORMERLY THE DEL RAY DREAMERY), 2310 MOUNT VERNON AVENUE

Admittedly, the Dairy Godmother—and its predecessor, the Del Ray Dreamery—is on the young side by classic restaurants standards, but its presence on Del Ray's main drag is so crucial and so beloved that it would be a sin not to recognize the impact it's had on the community over the years. Arriving on the scene in June 2001—just as the summer heat was really kicking in—the Del Ray Dreamery immediately solved a problem for Del Ray residents and visitors from all over town: Where to cool off with a custardy summer treat.

Founder and longtime owner Liz Davis came by the shop honestly.

*"I'm from Wisconsin, land of frozen custard," says Davis, 43, a former pastry chef. "I saw this gaping hole here that needed to be filled with a great dessert."*

*Her specialty is a "Wisconsin-style" dense, smooth frozen custard that is made in a special machine that she purchased for $50,000.*

*"At first it was confusing for people around here," she says. "They didn't understand that it's not a soft-serve ice cream with air beaten into it. There's no marshmallowy mouth feel." By USDA regulation, authentic frozen custard must be made with 10 percent butterfat and 1.4 percent egg yolk.[57]*

Certainly, Davis drew customers into the shop just by the simple fact that the Dreamery's smooth, slick custard was appealing enough. But more so, she piqued interest by the shop's interesting—and sometimes downright unique—flavor offerings, which change by the day. ("Cicada crunch," offered during the cicada-ridden summer of 2004, comes to mind.) While the classics never go out of style, the Dreamery has never been afraid to look further afield for inspiration.

In the mid-2000s, the Del Ray Dreamery was rebranded as the Dairy Godmother, but not much else changed; Davis remained at the helm and the custard kept coming out cold and refreshing. And not just for humans: Del Ray's dogs also came to expect their own flavors of canine custard, called Puppy Pops, just for them.

Near tragedy struck in 2017 when, after years of success (and the headaches of owning a small business), owner Davis decided to retire.

*"While the almost 17 years of owning The Dairy Godmother have brought me great joy, I will not be reopening in the spring," she wrote on the restaurant's website on Jan. 12. Davis has offered to sell the business, part and parcel, but will not be responding to communications until she returns from her hiatus abroad, she said.*[58]

The Alexandria community was bereft at the thought of losing such a storied shop, teeming with memories of summers (and falls, winters and springs) gone by. As the months ticked past, it seemed like the Dairy Godmother's days were behind it.

Until…

*"It took a long time to find the right person who is both a combination of heart and business knowledge," said Liz Davis, the Wisconsin native who founded the much-beloved sweet spot in the funky Alexandria neighborhood.*

*That person is Russell Gravatt, long a fixture in the area dining scene. He was involved with Amy's Ice Creams in Texas and helped found the original Austin Grill restaurant chain here.*

*"When I heard Liz was going to retire and take on the next stage of her life, I called her up and said, 'I'm interested,'" Russell said.*[59]

And with that, the Dairy Godmother was granted a reprieve. Gravatt had been a longtime fan of the shop; with his history in the restaurant industry, it only made sense for him to take over. Now, several years on, the shop hasn't skipped a beat, continuing to offer up custardy treats in all manner of flavors for Del Ray and beyond to enjoy.

*Said Liz: "His only flaw is he's not from Wisconsin. I think the customers are going to forgive him."*[60]

# Three

## Celebrating the Coast

With its proximity to the Potomac River and, extending outward, the Chesapeake Bay and Atlantic Ocean, it only makes sense that Alexandria would be a mecca of coastal cuisine. The menu extends much further than just crab cakes—all manner of seafood has been represented in the city's restaurants, from shrimp and oysters to a variety of fish.

While some restaurants have faced the cuisine in a more straightforward way, some have ventured further afield. A primarily seafood restaurant took on Cajun and Creole undertones once those flavored dishes began to resonate with the public. Another establishment ventured afield in a more physical way by building atop the Potomac River on pilings that kept it safe from the water. And some have kept the colonial spirit going by straddling the property that George Washington used to own. All of them are celebrating the coast in their own way—and with their own spin.

## THE SEAPORT INN, 6 KING STREET

Over the years, the Seaport Inn developed a certain fame of its own, but even in its humbler beginnings, it inherited a bit of notoriety because of the building that ensconced it. The restaurant may have opened its doors decades ago, but John Fitzgerald built his warehouse centuries prior, creating a linchpin of Alexandria's waterfront in the process.

Fitzgerald's Warehouse, as the site came to be known, came into being in the mid-1790s, a beneficiary of the filling-in of the Oronoco Bay that gave Alexandria's waterfront considerably more land to work with. It served many purposes and was home to several businesses over the years, but its restaurant history runs deep. As early as 1893, documents addressing "Brill's Restaurant" lend credence to the building's food-service history, "variously listed as a saloon, 'oysters and fish,' or, in 1924, as a lunchroom. Some of the name changes are doubtless due to Prohibition, in force in the 1920s."[61]

And lest one think the restaurant business was a boring and staid line of work, one has only to look at this snippet from the *Alexandria Gazette* in 1894 to be absolved of that idea: "A curiosity in the shape of a petrified ham is on exhibition at the restaurant of Mr. Jacob Brill. The ham was found in the ground near Staunton and will be sent to the Smithsonian Institution in Washington."[62]

By the time the Seaport Inn came on the scene in 1951, the Fitzgerald Warehouse had already seen quite a lot of life. Mr. and Mrs. Albert D. Schmutzer opened the restaurant as a more upscale, family-friendly

The Seaport Inn, pictured here in August 1955, became the newest resident of the Fitzgerald Warehouse in 1951. *Alexandria Library Local History Special Collections.*

The Seaport Inn's proximity to the Potomac River did occasionally have its drawbacks, such as during this heavy flood in 1972. *Alexandria Library Local History Special Collections.*

The former location of the Seaport Inn now plays host to several other businesses—most recognizably, a Starbucks. *Hope Nelson.*

*Left*: A plaque on the wall of the old Seaport Inn commemorates John Fitzgerald's contributions to the waterfront and to the city. *Hope Nelson.*

*Below*: This photo, taken from the corner of King and Union Streets, shows what a view of the landscape would look like during the Seaport Inn's lifetime. *Alexandria Library Local History Special Collections.*

alternative to the oyster bars (and presumably petrified ham exhibitions) of decades past and are "credited with helping reverse the long decline of the city's waterfront into which respectable folks seldom ventured."[63]

Over the coming years, the Seaport Inn continued its growth, both in terms of foot traffic as well as footprint; manager Paul Bynum, who became the restaurant's owner following Schmutzer's retirement in 1981, applied for and received a permit to construct an addition on the warehouse's east side in 1962 and, about fifteen years later, built a new kitchen for the facility as well.[64]

While the Seaport Inn continued forward in its growth, it also kept an eye on history.

*A plaque near the door of the Seaport Inn recounts Fitzgerald's accomplishments: aide-de-camp to General Washington, mayor of Alexandria, collector of the port under President John Adams. What it doesn't say—but what history records—is that Col. Fitzgerald rode for two years with Washington, froze with him at Valley Forge and rescued him at the Battle of Harlem Heights.*[65]

The Seaport Inn closed its doors for good in 2000, but its legacy isn't over. Indeed, the building remains today, as Old World as the day it was constructed, housing a Starbucks and a Thai restaurant—keeping the restaurant tradition alive for a third century. But visitors to the Seaport Inn would likely recognize the bones of the old place, persisting centuries after its emergence into Old Town's architectural culture.

## THE WAREHOUSE BAR AND GRILL, 214 KING STREET

At first blush, the Warehouse Bar and Grill is rather unassuming, situated as it is in the center of the 200 block of King Street, without a lot of fanfare to pull customers in. But peek inside; the dining room is pleasingly full, and there's a bustle coming and going from the kitchen. For more than thirty years now, this has been a popular go-to spot for higher-end seafood and steak dining, and business shows no sign of slowing.

The kid brother to Del Ray's RT's restaurant, the Warehouse was designed to be a little more upper crust, a little more fine dining in nature. (Think Alex P. Keaton to the rest of the *Family Ties* clan.) But stuffy it's not; rather, the restaurant has a down-to-earth feel amid the classiness.

The younger sibling to Arlandria's RT's, the Warehouse offers fine seafood dining with a Cajun twist. *Hope Nelson.*

Like its elder brother RT's, the Warehouse hews to the Cajun end of the spectrum, with beignets and oyster-loaf burgers leading the pack. And that hasn't changed. Consider *Washington Post* food reviewer Phyllis Richman's assessment in 1988, shortly after the restaurant opened:

> *Like its sibling, the Warehouse has a seafood emphasis and a New Orleans inclination. While blackened fish is no longer enough to identify a menu as Cajun/Creole (even La Colline serves blackened fish from its nouvelle French kitchen), the Warehouse also serves creole alligator stew, trout orleans, Cajun veal oscar and pasta jambalaya, in addition to smothering several dishes in hollandaise spiked with both scallions and creole mustard, as is the New Orleans habit.*[66]

Situated as it is on the heart of lower King Street, the Warehouse may be a longtime resident of 214 King, but it's certainly not the only one. Old editions of the *Alexandria Gazette* tout "Miss Mark's Seminary" offering courses at 214 in the 1860s,[67] and the Castner Electrolytic Alkali Company was in residence in the early 1900s (and hosted its shareholder meetings in the company headquarters in the building).[68] Like nearly every nook and cranny in the oldest part of Old Town, these buildings (as well as their predecessors) played host to all manner of businesses over the years.

But since 1988, the Warehouse has called 214 King Street home—with its own special blend of Cajun flair, both within the kitchen and outside of it.

> *The Warehouse, unlike RT's, was born with a silver spoon. After taking over a handsomely decorated site, it has enhanced it further. It is spacious and comfortable, with two main dining rooms, the front one a savvy combination of green velvet and marble, the rear room cozier and more like the French Quarter, with its striped wallpaper and patterned fabrics. But the delight of the Warehouse is at the entrance and up the staircase wall: a witty rogues' gallery of caricatures of local gentry.*[69]

For nearly three decades, Chef Sert Ruamthong has been at the restaurant's helm in the kitchen, churning out spicy, savory and sweet meals to generations of Alexandrians and visitors alike. And though the restaurant itself has a culinary angle, Ruamthong isn't afraid to call an audible where required.

*He says that Warehouse is a Cajun restaurant "but we make food the way you like it. And this is why I love it. Some people eat here 4–5 times a week, and if I know they are coming I know what they will want. But you feed 200–300 people a day that you don't know. Then you win when you figure it out."[70]*

## CEDAR KNOLL INN, 9030 LUCIA LANE

High atop a hill overlooking the Potomac River, nestled securely in the shadow of Mount Vernon, Cedar Knoll has kept watch over the George Washington Parkway and Mount Vernon Trail for decades. Save for a couple of intermissions, the historic restaurant has been in service since 1941, but the land it sits on has historic roots, as well.

George Washington purchased the land in 1760 and turned it into River Farm, one of Washington's five farm estates. The land was hived off and changed hands over the years, morphing into a plantation called Markland on the Potomac as well as the Mount Vernon View Antique Shop.[71]

By midcentury, Cedar Knoll was open and operating. "Perched above the George Washington Parkway a mile and a half north of Mount Vernon, the building originally was a tenant farmer's house for the mansion—now a religious retreat house—on George Washington's vast Riverbend Farm, and first opened as a restaurant in 1940."[72]

In terms of ambiance and décor, its storied history certainly gave the restaurant a leg up on the competition right off the bat. Even today, it's easy to envision oneself back in the 1700s, arriving for a fine meal perhaps via carriage, taking in the sights. "The white, wood-frame exterior and smoking brick chimneys have a gracious air about them as you approach the restaurant up its long drive, and the dark, wood-panelled interior, crimson ceiling, beams, detailed moldings and wall decorates such as pendulum clocks further the old-homestead atmosphere."[73]

As the years went on and tastes (and perhaps kitchen staff) changed, reviewers began to favor those architectural traits more than the food itself.

"Such a pretty white clapboard house set in a manicured garden edged with flowers! Such a stunning view of the river! You could leave it at that and not miss anything important," wrote *Post* food reviewer Phyllis Richman in 1977.[74]

But despite such occasional knocks, the restaurant carried on for several more decades, hosting everything from Easter dinners and wedding

Situated on a sprawling parcel of land, Cedar Knoll welcomes guests to a more pastoral setting. *Hope Nelson*.

The historic Cedar Knoll Inn has been on the outskirts of Alexandria since the mid-1900s. *Hope Nelson*.

Cedar Knoll continues to bring guests in from places near and far. *Hope Nelson.*

receptions to a romantic night out for two. But time finally caught up with the Cedar Knoll Inn.

The restaurant closed in November 2014 after a period of depletion and was put on the market shortly thereafter. Business partners Charlie Blevins, Andrew Holden and Chris Holden found their interest piqued by the listing and decided to dive in in an attempt to resurrect the fading historic business.

"Somebody should do something with that place," Andrew Holden remembers thinking of Cedar Knoll. "The area is starved for a great restaurant."[75]

The newest incarnation of Cedar Knoll has focused on American-style fare with a heavy emphasis on seafood—a natural choice given its proximity to the water. With the likes of ham-cured pork tenderloin, venison and jumbo lump crab cakes, one can imagine both diners from Washington's day as well as those of the modern era sitting down and digging in. Washington, though, may have been puzzled by the vegetarian wild mushroom tart.

And though its menu may have been modernized to suit changing twenty-first-century palates, one thing that hasn't changed much is the restaurant's interior, which harkens back to older times.

*With the property sitting on George Washington's river estate, Holden said there was no desire to modernize the restaurant's interior. Renovations included flooring, paint, antique decor and lighting, as well as a new exterior awning.*

*"We're entrenched in the history of the area," Holden said. "And we want the neighborhood to feel that this is their place. We are essentially a community restaurant here in Mount Vernon."[76]*

## BEACHCOMBERS RESTAURANT, 0 PRINCE STREET

Walk along the Potomac River through Old Town Alexandria in the mid-twentieth century, and it wasn't long before you would discover the Beachcombers Restaurant jutting out above the water. No, the building wasn't flooded; rather, its dining room was built on pilings that stood above the river, with a dock attaching the building to land.

The restaurant's beginnings were fairly straightforward. A newly constructed building when it first opened—a rarity among Old Town establishments, which generally bring with them a centuries-old pedigree—the Beachcomber was the brainchild of some well-known Alexandrians.

*In 1945, Clarence J. Robinson, founder of the Robinson Terminal Warehouse Corporation, leased a parcel east of the Strand at Prince Street to Edward Wayne, Thomas A. Hulfish Jr. and John Bethea, who planned to open a restaurant there. Construction soon began and within a year, the Beachcombers Restaurant, a two-story cinder block building, was built upon pilings in the Potomac.[77]*

It wasn't long before the restaurant opened its doors in 1946 to customers, many of whom reveled in the novelty of dining above the Potomac rather than adjacent to it. And the sight they beheld when they came in left them coming back for more.

*Customers accessed Beachcombers from a walkway and once inside, they could have dinner in the second floor dining room or outside. From a wraparound porch of the rooftop, patrons could enjoy a panoramic view of the Potomac and Maryland shore. Guests later recalled watching the evening ferry to Norfolk loading at the nearby dock. One frequent customer,*

Patrons of the Beachcombers Restaurant (shown here in 1948) could watch boats make their way up and down the Potomac River. *Alexandria Library Local History Special Collections.*

*Alice Roosevelt, the daughter of President Theodore Roosevelt, appreciated the view of lily pads and other aquatic plants.*[78]

Both the dock and the roof were memorable aspects of Beachcombers.

*Thomas Hulfish III, the owner's son, recalls that "all Alexandria came out at 7 to watch the Norfolk boat load (at the Prince Street dock). The stevedores sang sea chanties." On summer nights, pre-air-conditioning, "the dumb waiter took hard-shell crabs up to the roof, which was very attractive, decorated with lights."*[79]

From the famous guests to the regular workaday Alexandrians who popped in for a pint or a bite to eat, the restaurant was more than just its unique location. It offered a wealth of food, as well, mostly hewing to a coastal theme, given its strategic location. "In 1948…Beachcombers touted its fresh seafood and other specialties in newspaper ads, offering lobster supreme, full-bodied shrimp, steaks 'prepared to perfection' and a 'fine stock of imported and domestic wines and beer.'"[80]

And speaking of alcohol—as Beachcombers was situated above the water, it was rumored to be in Washington, D.C., rather than in Alexandria, as the District of Columbia owned the waterways at that time. Thus, the thinking was, the pub could stay open much later than all of Alexandria's other establishments. Some may debate the validity of the claim, but it surely helped sales. "On January 23, 1954, Beachcombers, vacant at the time, suffered significant damage in a fire. The owners decided to discontinue their restaurant business and sold the building later that year."[81]

The Beachcombers building wasn't completely destroyed by the fire, and though the incident marked the end of the restaurant's existence, it didn't mark the end of the building's life. The International Armaments Corporation moved in post-fire and launched the structure's decades-long status as a storage and retail space—and a source of a little tourism, too. "The building would be used by one owner or another for gun and ammunition storage and sales for the next fifty years, although in its later years the building's waterfront access would also allow dinner cruises to take place from its dock. It was sold to the City of Alexandria in 2006."[82]

A decade after the city took ownership of the space, in 2016, the structure was torn down in order to make room for the new Old Dominion Boat Club building, which opened in 2017.

# RT'S, 3804 MOUNT VERNON AVENUE

It's easy to miss the unassuming building featuring an Alexandria/Arlandria landmark as you tootle down Mount Vernon Avenue on your way to the Arlington border. But slow down and scan the left side of the street, your back to the Del Ray neighborhood, and there it sits: RT's, an Alexandria favorite for Cajun and seafood fare for more than thirty years.

Enter the vestibule and go on into the dining room, and nothing has changed there, either—but this is a feature, not a bug. RT's carved out its niche early on in the history of Mount Vernon Avenue, and its presence is clearly felt—and its popularity hasn't waned.

*Washington Post* food reviewers Mark and Gail Barnett couldn't stop raving about the restaurant shortly after its opening in 1985.

*All the more welcome, then, to RT's, a smashingly good little seafood restaurant where the sophistication is based on good sense and where,*

A hallmark of Mount Vernon Avenue for generations, RT's remains a warm and welcoming sight to enjoy seafood and Cajun fare. *Hope Nelson*.

The neon sign advertising RT's has been a longtime companion to the restaurant on the outskirts of Del Ray and Arlandria. *Hope Nelson.*

*remarkably, nearly all the improvised moves are the right ones. They really seem to understand a fundamental seafood axiom here: that a fish isn't a leg of lamb, that it can easily be overpowered by flavorings that are too intense or excessive. So RT's uses a light hand with the sauces and herbs—they're there to praise the food, not to bury it.*[83]

And within just a couple of years, *Post* food critic Phyllis Richman added it to her annual "50 Favorites" list, thereby putting it on the radar of foodies throughout the greater Washington region.

*This is an unflossy and attractive little restaurant with friendly service and comfortable booths, the kind of place you might be drawn to in nearly any mood. While half its main dishes are meat, it is known for its fish dishes with a Cajun accent. Its prices are modest, and if you stopped after the appetizers you would consider it a remarkable bargain. Oysters 3 Way is a mere $5.50 for half a dozen oysters in little ramekins of three different spicy buttery sauces. Steamed mussels are unique—as well as plentiful—in a pungent tomato sauce with sausage. And shrimp are agreeably prepared in a sherry-sweetened version of Russian dressing with impressive lumps of* *crab meat atop, or in the zesty Acadian peppered style that started in New Orleans' Italian restaurants.*[84]

With Ralph Davis at the helm, RT's took up shop in a building that had previously housed a pasta and pizza restaurant named Burnell's, which had enjoyed popularity but was beginning to take a turn for the worse. Couple that with a neighborhood that had seen its share of economic downturn itself, and Davis wasn't sure he wanted to make the move.

*But he had ownership on his mind and when, a few months later, he saw that plans were in the works to revitalize Mount Vernon Avenue, Ralph looked at Burnell's again.*

*"(Revitalization) was the reason I located here," he says. "I didn't realize it would start at the south end of the avenue and take more than 30 years."*[85]

Davis's faith in the business paid off, and while professional food critics weighed in with their opinions, local neighbors also became faithful friends over the years. And RT's also plays host to its share of celebrities and politicians—sometimes one and the same and sometimes not.

*Early on, RT's growing reputation and intimate venue attracted big names. No log exists, but they include: Sandra Day O'Connor, Sam Donaldson, Carl Bernstein, Dawn Wells (Mary Ann from* Gilligan's Island*), and many Birchmere headliners, most recently Steve Earle.*

*Also Kevin Bacon and Kris Kristofferson have made appearances. "But," says Davis, "our stock in trade is the politicians."*[86]

The Clintons and Gores dined at RT's in the early 1990s, and that opened the floodgates for a new generation of politicians of every stripe. Congressman Sonny Callahan entertained friends in the back room so often that it's been renamed the Callahan Room. Representative Mike Rogers and House Speaker John Boehner were regulars. And former House Speaker Paul Ryan has also been known to pop in from time to time.[87]

"For a hole in the wall on Mount Vernon Avenue," Davis told the *Zebra Press* in 2018, "I suspect we've had more Secret Service here than any restaurant in Alexandria."[88]

Politics aside, RT's is looking to the future. Davis's son, Matt, is a manager, and Ralph Davis is beginning to hand the reins over, slowly but surely. "If Matt wants to do this, I'd like RT's to continue for another generation. Business is on the uptick. And I'll tell you, when RT's captures people, we capture them. If they haven't eaten here, it's self-serving for me to say this, but 98 percent of the people who come here are very satisfied and they come back."[89]

## THE FISH MARKET, 105 KING STREET

For the past forty-plus years, the Fish Market on lower King Street has been an easy hallmark of Alexandria's port-city past, a reminder of the major economic interests that the city was founded on.

While the Fish Market opened in 1976, the building that houses it dates back much further. Originally a warehouse storing ships' cargo sailing in from all over the world, the structure then served as a field hospital for injured Confederate soldiers during the Civil War. In the early 1900s, it became the launchpad for a new soda called Chirp—"a bird of a drink," per the soda company's branding—and then, during Prohibition, it transitioned to harder carbonated beverages when it became a brewery. Along the way it also was used as a facility for curing meats of all kinds— and observant patrons will still see the nails used to hang beef and ham from the beams.[90]

Only in 1976 did it become the Fish Market that current visitors would know and love today. Launched by Ray Giovannoni—more popularly known as "Mr. Ray," also the namesake of Pop's ice cream—the Fish Market quickly became a go-to spot for fresh seafood and a menu of coastal favorites. Almost immediately, it drew the eye of the *Washington Post*.

> *The Fish Market is just that, but it also is a seafood restaurant with a raw bar. Its simple décor retains much of the old waterfront building it was when Alexandria was a seaport of note.*
>
> *The menu on a blackboard consists mainly of shellfish on the half shell and deep-fried; the same dishes are offered throughout the day, except crab imperial, which is served only at dinner. The list is repeated daily except for a fish of the day that may vary from croaker to sole or snapper.*[91]

The original iteration of the Fish Market was essentially a small sandwich counter with fewer than three dozen seats, but at its height the restaurant stretched all the way to Union Street. The schooners of beer also stretched

*Above*: At its largest, the Fish Market on King Street (shown here in August 1983) stretched all the way to Union Street. *Alexandria Library Local History Special Collections*.

*Right*: Originally a small counter with only about thirty seats, the Fish Market, pictured here in 1978, grew in size and scope over the years. *Alexandria Library Local History Special Collections*.

After the Landinis purchased the Fish Market in 2008, they renovated the restaurant to bring it up to more modern times. *Hope Nelson.*

nice and large, offering customers a thirty-two-ounce pour at any given time, and the cold schooner melded perfectly with the cold beer to provide refreshment no matter the season.

The early years of the Fish Market also offered up a piano bar as well as acoustic guitar entertainment to accompany the restaurant's simple menu of seafood favorites. A raw bar offered up some of the Atlantic's best shellfish and other rare fare.

Over the years, the Fish Market grew and shrank in size, causing the occasional stir with the city's Board of Architectural Review when it proceeded with construction in a way the city government did not like. But through it all, Giovannoni and his team continued to grow the popularity of the Fish Market, both with years-long regulars and visitors streaming in during Alexandria's tourist season.

Giovannoni died in May 1998 and left the Fish Market to his son, wife and a handful of employees. A decade later, in 2008, Franco and Noe Landini purchased the restaurant and set to work renovating the space to bring it up to the standards of the new millennium. At first, this raised concerns from the Fish Market's faithful, but in due time the furor settled down and the perked-up version of the restaurant began to win customers over once more.[92]

*The Landinis immediately gutted the place, took out a bar, and rebuilt the entire place including a new and modern kitchen. Cory Fey, now the Corporate Executive Chef, was brought in to run the kitchen and he added more items to the list of fried, broiled or steamed fish choices. Today, the restaurant offers a raw bar, soups and chowders, starters and salads, sandwiches, burgers & tacos, grilled platters, fried platters, specialties, nautical pastas, sides and a kid's menu. The menu is very extensive but many favorites have remained over the years.[93]*

With a spiced-up facelift, a renewed menu that kept the popular favorites while introducing some new flavors and the same casual coastal vibe as ever, the Fish Market is poised to proceed for many more decades as one of Alexandria's most popular, beloved seafood restaurants and raw bar. Perch at one of the balcony tables and lift a schooner of beer to all that has passed and all yet to come.

# THE WHARF, 119 KING STREET

By now, it should come as no surprise that the 100 block of King Street is a treasure-trove of historic buildings that have shouldered a multitude of purposes over the years. The building that sits at 119 King Street, near the top of the block, is no outlier. Thought to be constructed in the 1790s, the structure where the Wharf now sits had as much of a storied past as its neighbors.

*One of the first businesses in the new building was the Miller Company, described in history books as "importers and dealers in crockery, china, etc..." The Miller Company installed an elevator, the lift of which can still be seen next to the bar next to the restaurant and the pulley wheels in the attic.*[94]

The building sold at auction in 1885 for $3,000, and after that it saw an address change—from "No. 27 King Street, 60 feet East of Water Street" to the now-familiar 119 King Street, which it has remained ever since.[95] It then became a feed and grain warehouse, like so many other structures near the water in Old Town, before, much later, becoming the Wharf restaurant in 1972.

*The restaurant occupies premises that once were a warehouse built in about 1800. Original roughly hewn columns and beams have been retained, along with stone and brick construction and an ancient freight elevator. Cargo nets, pulleys and rope abound. All this provides a pleasing ambience, along with well-spaced and varnished tables with proper settings of cutlery.*[96]

Known for its seafood, the Wharf became known just as well for its music scene. The bar upstairs, the Quarter Deck, quickly became popular as a club, drawing the eye of food reviewers almost as much as the cuisine did:

*At the Quarter Deck you can hear a live band and speak in a normal tone of voice at the same time. It's dimly lit, but not so dim that you can't see the face across from you. It's comfortable, with dark wood, brick walls and a friendly atmosphere. Customers are as willing to share tables as opinions.*

*If old salts were still tying up at the docks only a block away, they'd feel right at home with the harpoon hanging from the ceiling and the four-foot-wide rudder above the doorway. (Advice for the very tall: duck.)*[97]

*Left*: The building that now houses the Wharf began its life as an importer of china and other home goods. *Hope Nelson*.

*Below*: The Wharf, pictured here in 1983, has had a long and storied history in Old Town Alexandria. *Alexandria Library Local History Special Collections*.

The Wharf (and Landini Brothers) features prominently in this 1979 view of the 100 block of King Street. *Alexandria Library Local History Special Collections.*

A drawback to living on lower King Street is the pervasive flooding that creeps up the road after a heavy rain, tropical storm or other special weather event. The Wharf fell prey to these sorts of scenes, too, even when the rest of Old Town wasn't paying attention (or was too busy partying).

> *A crowd of about 100 milled around drinking cocktails as the Potomac River rose slowly above Union Street and inched its way toward a row of shops below South King Street—and toward the party.*
>
> *"I guess we're the only people in Alexandria doing anything (about the floods),"said [co-owner Cliff] Cline. In front of the restaurant below, a three-foot high cinderblock wall filled with sand and covered with tar stood to guard against any water moving up the street.*[98]

The Wharf changed hands in 1997, just in time for the twenty-first century, its fourth decade of life. After that, it has continued to rumble right along, delighting new generations of diners from its vantage point in one of the most historic blocks in Old Town.

# Four

# Alexandria's International Hot Spots

A t first blush, the seaport city doesn't exactly seem like it would be a bustling repository of international cuisine. But peel back the curtain a little more and it's easy to see a thriving community of multicultural cuisine at work throughout town.

From French stalwarts to spicy, refined Indian dishes served in a basement dining room, the city has grown into a diverse community representing a colorful palette of cuisines. Mexican, Latin American, European, African… it's all here. The city offers up a rainbow of flavors behind its numerous dining-room doors. All that visitors and residents have to do is go out and taste them.

## LA TRATTORIA (NÉE TRATTORIA DA FRANCO), 300 SOUTH WASHINGTON STREET

To walk into this little Italian café just south of King Street is to take a step back in time—in all the right ways. Less dated, more date-night, La Trattoria has for decades been an Alexandria fixture—for both its food and the faces who work and dine there.

La Trattoria is a new name for a decades-old staple of Old Town cuisine. Beginning life as Trattoria da Franco—an homage to its founder and longtime chef and owner, Franco Abbruzzetti—the trattoria first opened

Trattoria da Franco—now La Trattoria—has been a vibrant presence on Washington Street for decades. *Hope Nelson.*

in 1972 and continued life uninterrupted for more than forty years until Abbruzzetti's retirement. But by then, Trattoria da Franco had wormed its way into the hearts of Alexandrians past and present with its food, its ambiance and its opera.

Wait. Opera?

Opera. For years, the trattoria has hosted an opera night on the final Sunday of each month; patrons are invited to eat and drink as per usual but with the added benefit of an operatic singer crooning Italy's best songs.

From the music to the cuisine, Abbruzzetti made patrons feel right at home from day one of the trattoria's existence. Just walking outside the eatery on South Washington Street, diners knew they were in for a homey treat. As Phyllis Richman wrote in the *Washington Post* in 1987:

> *Some restaurants have a head start before you're even shown to your table. Trattoria da Franco is one. Outside, the front window and awning identify it as a small and personal place, and the blackboard with the daily specials reinforces that spirit. Inside, there appear to be, at most, a dozen tables, though an attractive dining room upstairs is ready to catch any overflow. A host or hostess greets you with enthusiasm, and likely as not the chef is*

*chatting with the diners, showing photographs of his father's restaurant in Rome or describing the dish he thinks they should have. A diner returning for a second visit may be greeted with a hug as an old friend; a birthday celebrant gets the full-staff chorus singing in Italian.*

*Trattoria da Franco is the kind of Italian restaurant where you'd expect the young Dean Martin to have come every Sunday with his parents.*[99]

Person by person, table by table would sit down and soak in the family-style environment; you were always at home at Franco's. Along with visits by Abbruzzetti himself, the waitstaff also became a long-tenured force of nature, becoming part of the fabric of the restaurant as the years ticked by. To say nothing of the food: Homemade bread, rich, thick pasta and hearty sauces won the day, serving as a proper complement to the restaurant's extensive wine list.

*The key to enjoying Trattoria da Franco is tomatoes. At every meal, the tomato sauce was the standout of the cookery. And chef Franco Abbruzzetti seems to know that. As I watched and listened, he always recommended dishes with tomato sauce. And even when we ordered a veal in cream sauce he sent out one with tomato sauce—thank goodness.*[100]

Over time, as the restaurant and Abbruzetti continued to age, the illustrious Franco prepared to bid the business farewell. But what to do? To close outright, or to hope for a buyer to carry on the culinary traditions well into the twenty-first century? The answer came in the form of a longtime patron, Michael Strutton, a rookie to the restaurant game but a longtime entrepreneur.

*"I've been coming here for years as a customer; pretty much every Saturday night I came here for probably five years. I'm extremely involved in my Italian culture, so this was to me in Old Town as close as I could get to that as far as food, and just a vintage experience which I appreciate more than trendy or 'fad' type dining," he said. "I knew that Franco had ideas of retiring or selling, and I knew that this place was underperforming and really needed an injection of energy and vision…and so it was just always on my mind."*

*When Abbruzzetti did list the restaurant with a broker, Strutton made his intentions known. And after months of negotiation and legalities, La Trattoria emerged in its new form.*[101]

The interior of the former Trattoria da Franco was updated after the restaurant changed hands, but the cozy dining room remains just as warm and welcoming. *Hope Nelson.*

From its early days under Franco de Abbruzetti, Trattoria da Franco (now La Trattoria) made sure that white-tablecloth service didn't get in the way of down-home Italian cooking. *Hope Nelson.*

La Trattoria continues the plan set out for it by Abbruzzetti: good food, extensive wine list, fair prices. Even much of the kitchen staff and waitstaff have carried over from Franco's day. And the opera night is just where you'd expect it: every fourth Sunday, like clockwork.

## LE GAULOIS, 1106 KING STREET

For years, the wooden gargoyles keeping watch on either side of the front door welcomed visitors into Le Gaulois, a venerable French restaurant smack-dab in the middle of King Street's Old Town blocks. The kid sibling of a restaurant by the same name in Washington, D.C., Le Gaulois came to Alexandria in 1988 and maintained its reign in the city until 2009, when the restaurant closed its doors.

Its arrival in Old Town caused quite a stir. The original outpost in the District was known for its formidable French fare, and residents as well as food reviewers jumped at the chance to try out the newcomer's menu.

> *The menu is familiar to Gaulois-watchers. The regular dishes (appetizers such as ratatouille, snails, duck pate' and onion soup; "cuisine minceur" of steamed and foil-baked fish, veal and chicken; and entrees such as omelets, quiches, crepes and meat salads) are supplemented by a long list of specials. The prices are still moderate, and the seasonal specialties—several creamy vegetable soups, soft-shell crabs amandine, zucchini "spaghetti" with seafood, veal with fresh raspberry sauce, swordfish with basil and tomato—refresh winter-jaded appetites.*[102]

One thing that stood out about Le Gaulois was its array of less-available (some might argue less-popular to American palates, though there was certainly a fan base) French finds, such as "brains in vinaigrette."[103]

> *At Le Gaulois in Alexandria, the quenelles are of the same extraordinary quality* [as the D.C. location]. *Recently, while speaking with the chef there, Raymond Gayet, I complimented him on his quenelles, calling them comparable to those at Nandron. His face lit up as he proudly informed me that he had served his apprenticeship in the kitchens of Nandron.*[104]

The wooden gargoyles at Le Gaulois, pictured here circa 1990, kept watch over King Street for many years. *Alexandria Library Local History Special Collections*.

The site of Le Gaulois is now poised to become a Belgian mussel house. *Hope Nelson*.

Le Gaulois, the sign pictured here circa 1990, came to Alexandria in 1988 and stayed for more than two decades. *Alexandria Library Local History Special Collections.*

Even in a city where Old World architecture is a prized characteristic, Le Gaulois stood out. From the gargoyles to the brick-walled interior, from the white tablecloths to the open and airy dining room, Le Gaulois brought an air of something new—yet also older, wiser in all the best ways—to the neighborhood. A patio took up residence adjacent to the interior space, providing diners with a wonderfully tree-shaded respite from the summer heat and a lovely place to dine in springtime or autumn.

Indeed, Le Gaulois stood the test of several decades, finally closing its doors in 2009. Since its closure, the site has seen a parade of restaurants come and go, ranging from wine bars to steakhouses. Now, a Belgian mussel house is making a go of it. The gargoyles' spirit still looks on.

## DISHES OF INDIA, 1510-A BELLEVIEW BOULEVARD

Smack-dab on the border between Alexandria city and Fairfax County sits a spicy Indian restaurant in an unlikely location. Pull up to the shopping center at Belleview Boulevard, and it's not immediately apparent that one of the region's very best Indian eateries resides within it. Rather, it takes a leap of faith, a pull of a door and a venture down a staircase to find the basement enclave—but once you do, you know you're in for a treat.

Dishes of India began its life in June 1997, the brainchild of Chef Ramanand Bhatt, who began his career at sixteen in a roadside café in India and had always dreamed of opening his own restaurant someday. After years of working in others' kitchens and with others' food, he made the leap and christened Dishes of India several blocks from the Potomac River.

The storefront of Dishes of India may be rather plain, but the restaurant's food livens things up. *Hope Nelson.*

What the location lacked in view—it is a basement, after all—it made up for immediately in taste as well as hospitality. The *Washington Post*'s Domenica Marchetti wrote in 2001:

> *No matter that the smallish dining room lacks a window, or that the pink wallpaper is slightly frayed and faded—left over from the locale's previous incarnation as a seafood restaurant. What Dishes of India lacks in decor it more than makes up for in great food, impeccable service and welcome touches of civility not usually found in modest establishments....*
>
> *The wait staff, too, is unfailingly courteous, and food is presented with care. "Service, cleanliness, quality, those are the things that are important to us," said [co-owner and manager Naresh] Bhatt, whose father, Ramanand Bhatt, is the chef. "So many friends and relatives told us we were making a mistake opening in this location. But my father and I decided to take this challenge. If you have quality and atmosphere, the people will come back."*[105]

This staircase leads diners to the delicacies that come from Dishes of India's kitchen. *Hope Nelson.*

In a shopping center, Dishes of India's patrons head straight downstairs to the basement. *Hope Nelson.*

The dining room's hospitality quickly gives way to the food, which is Indian cuisine at its very best. From the tandoor oven, piping hot at 500 degrees, to the slew of biryani dishes, the kitchen turns out one good item after another—often to a jam-packed space. A hidden gem, this is not; anyone in the region with a grasp on good Indian food has this location circled on their map, big and red.

*My absolute favorite dish is the began bartha ($7.95 for lunch, $8.95 for dinner), a vegetarian specialty of roasted eggplant mashed together with a rich, buttery sauce of tomato and onions. It's perfect spooned over a mound of saffron and cinnamon-infused basmati rice, or even better, scooped up with a wedge of naan—soft, chewy flat bread baked in the tandoor.*[106]

The Bhatts have made Dishes of India a family affair. Chef Ramanand has enlisted his sons to run the restaurant since its opening, and with great success—but not without struggles. In 2003, the dining room fell victim to the flooding left behind after Hurricane Isabel. Though Ramanand Bhatt initially didn't want to rebuild, the family carried the day; the restaurant opened its doors again once the floodwaters receded, and Dishes of India was brought back to its former glory. The customers were ready and waiting.

And speaking of those customers: They fan out nationwide. "One couple was so enamored of the place that when they moved to New Mexico, they packed a carryout meal from the restaurant and brought it on their flight. Then they sent Bhatt a postcard to say that the meal had arrived safely and was delicious. Bhatt has saved the postcard, along with stacks of comment cards that diners are encouraged to fill out."[107]

There's not a much greater tribute than that.

## TAQUERIA POBLANO, 2400 MOUNT VERNON AVENUE

By classic restaurants standards, Del Ray's Taqueria Poblano is a baby of the group. The Baja California–styled taco joint is only two decades old, coming on the scene in 1999, but over the years it has become an institution within Alexandria's international food scene. But to label it a straight Mexican restaurant would be a vast misnomer. Rather, the tacos this kitchen produces are a healthy blend of Mexican and Californian stylings, providing diners with the best of both cultures on one pastel-colored plate.

> *Cal-Mex cuisine, just like its black-sheep cousin, Tex-Mex, has its apologists and its detractors. The critics, of course, deride the food for not being regional Mexican cooking, as though geography has no influence on how one puts together a meal. Cal-Mex shares another quality with the Texas branch of the family, too: It's hard to define in any scholarly or even satisfactory way.*[108]

The taqueria was a much-needed addition to Del Ray's restaurant scene when it arrived just before the dawn of the twenty-first century. A small space, Taqueria Poblano feels less cramped and more cozy. The

Taqueria Poblano—shown here as a former tenant, Mac's Place—has become a mainstay in Del Ray. *Alexandria Library Local History Special Collections*.

The patio at Taqueria Poblano often has an hourlong wait on seasonable days. *Hope Nelson*.

décor has always helped, as well. From a *Washington Post* review on the heels of its opening:

> *It might be dark and cold outside, but Taqueria Poblano bids its guests welcome with a modestly sunny dining room. Tiny white lights frame the picture window. The walls are bathed in terra-cotta hues and dressed up with sconces and pictures, souvenirs picked up during trips to Mexico by [owner Glen] Adams and his wife and partner, Karen Kowalczyk.*[109]

The outside of the restaurant is just as friendly—and just as cozy—as the inside. Seating for close to half a dozen tables is available on the restaurant's "front porch," as it were, overlooking Del Ray's main drag, Mount Vernon Avenue. At all times of the year, the porch is full to bursting with diners—and would-be diners in waiting—who are enjoying either the spring or summer weather…or who are nestled among stand-up heaters, a plastic sheet enclosing the space somewhat.

Where many taco-centric eateries focus on the Mexican side of the border, Taqueria Poblano has always managed to hew to a more diversified feel. The "L.A.-style crispy tacos" have been a mainstay at the restaurant since its opening, and most of the menu items soundly straddle the border between North and Central America. But "don't come expecting Mexican fast food that is Americanized in a cloak of cheese or loaded on a combo platter (thank goodness)," *Washington Post* food critic Tom Sietsema writes.[110] He's right about that.

The Taqueria Poblano family has continued to grow in the twenty years since Adams began the Del Ray outpost. Both the locations as well as the menu have grown and changed to adapt to new palate (and residency) demands.

> *Certainly Adams has memories of specific California-oriented Mexican dishes, from burritos to crispy tacos, that he brought to life at Poblano. But in the 14 years since launching his taqueria, he has expanded not only its presence, with two more locations in Arlington County, but also its menu. Aside from tributes to Cal-Mex tacos and burritos, Poblano serves up dishes influenced by regional Mexican cooking, whether from the Yucatan (an achiote-rubbed steak Tampiqueno) or Oaxaca (a chicken mole verde).*[111]

Though its menu has adapted with the times, the Del Ray mainstay remains the favorite it became almost immediately upon opening—a true classic, even at a mere twenty years old.

# CHEZ ANDRÉE, 10 EAST GLEBE ROAD

To be sure, Chez Andrée remains one of Alexandria's most well-known French restaurants, even several years after its closure. Beginning life in 1964, the restaurant served customers for more than a half century prior to shutting its doors in 2015.

Chez Andrée prided itself on being acutely French—not "French and." And with such a strict devotion to its chosen cuisine, it garnered favor regionwide—and maintained it throughout its tenure.

*No "fusion" dishes pairing French and Asian ingredients, no presentations so stunning or sculpted that they look like they belong in an art gallery rather than on a dinner plate. Just solid French fare such as steak au poivre, fresh calf's liver sauteed with onions, rainbow trout with almonds, and the like.*

*And that's the way it's going to stay, co-owner Laurence Matrat promises.*

*"We do good, hearty, authentic French cooking," she said. "Not too many places do that anymore."*[112]

The restaurant lived its entire life there on East Glebe Road, on the outskirts of Del Ray and bordering Arlandria. Opened by Matrat's parents, Stanley and Andrée Lecureux, the restaurant never strayed from its original focus—though it did grow its footprint, from a one-room, two-dozen-seat affair to a building with three dining rooms and availability to accommodate more than one hundred people at a time.

*Mr. Lecureux, who worked for United Airlines in 1964, got in the habit of dropping by a nearby bar in Alexandria for a burger and beer—and conversation—with the Parisian-born barmaid. The two hit upon the idea of buying a restaurant, so shortly before they married, they purchased a small establishment called the Auburn Bar and Grill, which was near the railroad yard. Its location was less than promising for any kind of eating establishment.*

*They kept the old bar sign, "Shirt and Shoes Required," started serving French specials twice a week and changed the name to Chez Andrée, after Mr. Lecureux's wife, who was the chef. Thanks in part to a thumbs-up review by a restaurant critic, the lines soon were long, the bar was gone and the restaurant was thriving.*[113]

Opening its doors in 1964, Chez Andrée served customers for more than a half century prior to closing in 2015. A new restaurant, Northside 10, has taken its place. *Hope Nelson.*

Before too long, the secret was out about Chez Andrée, and the restaurant began attracting people from around the region to come enjoy its traditional French comfort food. From fish dishes to New York strip steak to duck à l'orange and, yes, escargots and liver, the eatery ran the gamut of delicacies, both from within Paris and without.

> *Perhaps what's most appealing about Chez Andrée is its steadfast allegiance to traditional, unpretentious cuisine.*
>
> *"People come here because they feel at home," Matrat said. "Why would we change that?"*[114]

In the mid-1990s, Stanley and Andrée retired and turned the restaurant over to their children, Laurence Matrat and Steve Lecureux, who remained at the helm until the restaurant closed in October 2015. Now a new dining spot, Northside 10, has taken up residence, offering a more American take on cuisine, but still hewing to the comfortable, homey restaurant that launched 10 East Glebe all those years ago.

Five
# Memorable Renegades

Everybody loves an eccentric, and these food purveyors—restaurants, groceries and markets all—are some of Alexandria's most beloved outside-the-box thinkers. What does a gregarious Irishman have in common with a grocery store that brought new kinds of food to the city for the first time? How has an open-air market survived three centuries of change, upheaval and occasional near-death experiences? Has a cursed building finally found its savior?

Alexandria is full of unique characters. Some are human, some are establishments and some are beautiful buildings and market squares that have overseen the growth, development and mishaps of the city. But one thing is for certain: Each of these memorable renegades is beloved in its own way.

## PAT TROY'S IRELAND'S OWN, 132 NORTH ROYAL STREET/123 NORTH PITT STREET

Any Alexandrian worth calling the city home knows the name Pat Troy. The gregarious Irishman was a fixture at all manner of events, parades and even the local city council ballot on occasion. But what Troy was most known for was his longstanding Irish pub that called two addresses home over the course of decades—Ireland's Own.

*Above*: Pat Troy's Ireland's Own called several addresses home over the years, but Troy made sure to spread the love no matter his restaurant's location. *Alexandria Library Local History Special Collections.*

*Right*: The final site of Pat Troy's became a burger restaurant after the Irish pub closed. Now it awaits its next tenant. *Hope Nelson.*

After arriving in the United States in 1962, it didn't take Troy long to set up housekeeping. Gregarious to a fault and always up for a good story, Troy set to work making connections that would lead him to his life's work.

> *Mr. Troy soon headed to where "all the diplomats, all the presidents" live, in Washington, where he was hired by Count Andre Marie Adrian de Limur, a pilot in the French Flying Corps. He worked as a butler for Count de Limur and his wife, Ethel Crocker, for three years, during which time he met such people as Stuart Davidson, founder of Clyde's restaurants, and actor Maurice Chevalier.*
>
> *The Irish butlers in Washington were a close-knit group, Mr. Troy said, and could be relied upon for a job well done. His connections within the community led him to working dinners at Robert F. Kennedy's house and rubbing elbows with past presidents at the F Street Club, where he introduced himself to Presidents Eisenhower and Truman and renowned aviator Charles A. Lindbergh.*
>
> *He became a U.S. citizen in 1967, a day Mr. Troy said he counts as one of the most memorable of his life.*
>
> *"When that woman handed me my first American flag…that was a great feeling for me."*[115]

In 1973, he and his wife, Bernadette, took ownership of the Irish Walk gift shop on King Street, but their business careers were just beginning. By the mid-1970s, Troy had launched his Old Town establishment, which quickly became a hub of civic life. A staunch Republican and devoted Catholic, Troy used his restaurant to cater to political and religious causes that were dear to him. But regardless of party or religious affiliation, everyone was welcome (and at home) in Ireland's Own.

It was perhaps Troy's political persuasion that led President Ronald Reagan to make a visit one St. Patrick's Day in 1988, to the delight (and shock) of both staff and diners.

> *At Ireland's Own, the pub in Old Town Alexandria, Reagan arrived with White House Chief of Staff Howard Baker, syndicated columnist James J. Kilpatrick and sculptor Marie Pietri, Kilpatrick's wife. A table had been reserved for Baker.*
>
> *"But we didn't know until five minutes before he got here that the president was coming," said Bunty Dornan, an assistant to pub owner Pat Troy.*

*Reagan's 45-minute stay sent 300 pub patrons into a frenzy of singing and clapping to Irish songs and telling Irish jokes. The president joined for a verse of "When Irish Eyes Are Smiling." Belfast tenor Seamus Kennedy was the featured act but quickly made way for an old pro at scene-stealing who had a couple of gags of his own to tell.*[116]

Though Washington luminaries like Reagan felt at home there, the pub was no stuffy environment for locals. Warm and inviting—but rather a stranger to the sun—the original bar on Royal Street nearly always had a gaggle of patrons, no matter the day (or the comfortable climate outside). Pubgoers looking for the best of both worlds took up residence on the patio.

Ireland's Own had a lengthy tenure on North Royal Street. A fixture of Tavern Square, patrons were concerned when the building Ireland's Own resided in was sold and rents shot up. Troy's search for a new location became a citywide debate. One leading potential location, at 100 North Lee Street, sparked the ire of Torpedo Factory Condo Association members, who "protested the move and distributed flyers, which included such statements as 'Ireland's Own is not just a bar; it's an Irish bar.'"[117]

When all was said and done, Ireland's Own moved just across the Tavern Square courtyard to 123 North Pitt Street, keeping the familiar alongside the new and novel. With the move, Ireland's Own became Pat Troy's Restaurant and Pub, but while the name and location may have shifted, the feel of the restaurant remained very much the same, right down to the Guinness and corned beef and cabbage.

After the move in March 2000, Pat Troy's went on to enjoy another fourteen years of success, first with Troy at the helm and then under the guidance of his longtime employees Margaret Keane and Scott Holdt. In 2013, though, Holdt and Keane filed for Chapter 11 bankruptcy. By 2014, the pub had closed its doors for good.

*Troy, disappointed in the state of his old pub, is not shy about saying he would have done things differently. At his retirement party in 2012, he made it clear he wanted to continue playing a role in the business. Looking back, he wishes his successors had taken him up on the offer.*

*"It's a sad way to see it going* [out of business] *when it should be going for another 33 years," Troy said. "In my 34 years, I had great memories of that place. It went so fast."*[118]

Pat Troy died in March 2018, just days after serving as the grand marshal of his beloved St. Patrick's Day parade in Alexandria.

> *"What a great way to go," [Magee] Whelan said. "That he was able to be, with his beautiful bride Bernadette at his side, that they were able to be grand marshals of the parade this past Sunday, and give his last big shout out, 'Erin go Bragh' [Ireland forever] and then three days later, he's dead. What a high. What a super swan song."*
>
> *"He walked out of the door to the parade, and we pray, walked into another parade in heaven not much long after that," said the Rev. Edward Hathaway, rector of Troy's parish, the Basilica of St. Mary.*[119]

# MISHA'S, 102 SOUTH PATRICK STREET AND 917 KING STREET

Visitors to Misha's Coffee Roaster and Coffeehouse can oftentimes smell the shop before they see it; the pungent, thick aroma of roasted coffee beans permeates the air and even wafts outside, beckoning Alexandria's tired masses to perk up with a cup of hand-crafted joe.

An Old Town mainstay since it opened in 1991, Misha's was launched by Misha Von Elmendorf and Andrea Seward and was quickly embraced by the community as a locally owned, anti–big business establishment. The wide array of coffee beans available—to say nothing of the sweet treats under glass cloches on the counter—didn't hurt its popularity, either.

> *"I think we are unique, we are not a chain. We bring authenticity" said Seward in reference to the coffeehouse. And that is a trait the customers seem to like. Brian McDonald, a customer, said "I think it is an anti-Starbucks sort of bohemian."*
>
> *Kait Neely, a regular customer, said the area is "lacking in cool coffee shops, but I like this one."*
>
> *With hand picked and high end coffee beans making their way from places all over the world into this locally owned coffee shop, Seward said "we are artist coffee roasters."*[120]

Longtime customers will remember that, for many years, the scent of roasting beans blended with cigarette smoke; the 2009 smoking ban dispensed with such blends, delighting some customers and dismaying others. But Misha's continued on post-cigarette, and its empire continues to grow, its identity deepening.

It doesn't take long for visitors to recognize the individuality of Misha's. A cookie-cutter coffeeshop this is not—and it's all for the better.

*Misha's has a relaxed, artsy feel to it, with colorful red, yellow and blue walls and a menu spelled out in children's refrigerator magnets. It's a great place to stop for a little caffeine pick-me-up or liquid relief from the Old Town summer heat, but it's also a nice place to spend some time alone or with friends over a cup of fresh, bold coffee. On any weekday morning, the cafe is abuzz with commuters en route to the District. Weekends are more relaxed with children and pets in tow. Alexandria is a dog-lovers town, and you're sure to find a few of man's best friends chilling outside in the morning sun.*[121]

But a cult classic Misha's isn't. Rather, it's attracted neighbors, tourists and other visitors from all walks of life, from the famous to the private citizen to everyone in between.

*Big names such as Sen. Mark Warner (D-Va.) and former Speaker Newt Gingrich (R-Ga.) and his wife, Callista, have visited Misha's in the past, but Seward said she and her co-owner (Misha, himself) have never dwelled upon the occasional presence of D.C. celebrities within their walls. The employees and owners of Misha's are interested in every customer that comes in, not just the ones who might later appear on C-SPAN.*[122]

Nearly thirty years on from its opening, 2019 brought with it quite a lot of change for the storied coffee shop. For the first time since its birth, Misha's has moved—leaving the confines of its well-known Route 1 location and instead rounding the corner to set up shop on also-well-known King Street. The storefront is certainly different—rather than a rectangular expanse stretching down the block, it is neatly nestled into a row of shops in the 900 block of King—but its aura and vibe continue to be inherently Misha's-esque. The move hasn't stripped the coffeehouse of its identity, even though the square footage is larger and the shop appears to have "grown up."

And the growth hasn't stopped there—as of this writing, Misha's continues to eye a second location closer to the waterfront, just around the corner from Chadwick's. And one thing is for certain: Old Towners certainly aren't complaining about the possibility for more coffee in their lives.

# CASH GROCER, 1315 KING STREET

Well before organic foods were de rigueur, there was Cash Grocer, a warm, earthy natural-foods grocery store keeping watch over the upper blocks of King Street. The shop was well ahead of its time, offering up all manner of "hippie" fare and personal care items in an era when the city was largely big-box and big-business.

Cash Grocer opened in what was originally a private home constructed in 1804. Fagelson's Toy Store took up residence in the mid-twentieth century, and in the 1960s, the home became the Casablanca Bar, "touting the longest bar on the East Coast."[123] Within another decade or so, Cash Grocer moved in, with owner Peggy Kleysteuber moving in above the shop in a small apartment on the second floor.

Kleysteuber, an Alexandria native, initially opened Cash Grocer in 1975, first on North Pitt Street and then at the King Street location that so many neighbors became accustomed to over the years.

> *In fact, the name for the store "Cash Grocer" came from an artifact Kleysteuber found in her grandfather's basement. It was a small leaded glass sign that read Cash Grocer. "I don't know where it came from, but I liked it, so that's how I named the store," she said. She then had a large stained glass window made to resemble the small sign and installed it as part of the store's front window.*[124]

That window was what often led passersby to investigate the shop further. And what they found was a treasure-trove. Early on, the concept of "natural foods" was so out of the normal modus operandi for neighbors that they really had no idea what they were walking in on. And even once organic produce and natural personal care products had begun to find their niche in the national landscape, Cash Grocer offered up goods that none of the larger retailers were providing.

> *"We moved here from the Bronx in 1972. When Peggy opened I popped in just out of curiosity. I walked in and I walked out. Then I walked back in. I didn't understand all that stuff she was selling," [customer Jackie] Spegai said.*
>
> *"I didn't know anything about the various foods so I asked if she had distilled water. She asked me why I wanted distilled water. I said isn't that supposed to be good for you? Her answer was, 'No—it's dead water,'" Spegai recalled.*

Cash Grocer Natural Foods, the sign pictured here circa 1990, was one of the first grocery stores in Alexandria to bring organic and so-called health foods to neighbors. *Alexandria Library Local History Special Collections.*

Now, the former site of Cash Grocer plays host to a twenty-four-hour fitness center. *Hope Nelson.*

*"That started our friendship and my knowledge of macrobiotics. There are just so many people from all walks of life throughout the entire area that shop in that store. Peggy truly embraced the natural food way of life,"* she said.

*"Peggy is and has been unique. I'm a different person because of the Cash Grocer and Peggy,"* Spegai exclaimed.[125]

Walking into the shop was always a feast for the senses. The smells of herbs and incense wafted past customers' noses as soon as they entered the store, and the rich hues of organic vegetables called out for further investigation. The macrobiotic and health-food wares were always intriguing; often, Cash Grocer was the only shop in the city that carried such specialty brands and goods.

"Most of things we carry are just not sold in the large chain stores," Kleysteuber told the *Alexandria Gazette Packet* in 2007.[126]

But despite Cash Grocer's domination of the health-foods niche, the large chains began to eat away at the little shop's market share, and by the time the mid-2000s rolled around, it was clear to Kleysteuber that the end was nigh. By August 2007, she had sold the entire building and was liquidating, much to the dismay of a passel of faithful longtime customers. But Kleysteuber said she just couldn't keep up the fight against the larger businesses, no matter how vibrant her customer base was.

*"I can no longer compete with the large chain stores. They get much better deals from the manufacturers than a small store like mine..."*

*"It's the same thing that's happening to all small businesses. And, it will continue to happen unless the city is willing to provide some form of protection to small businesses,"* she said.[127]

Cash Grocer's former location now sports a twenty-four-hour gym. Though its façade has been overhauled, longtime Alexandrians still can't help but spy a shadow of the former stained glass out of the corner of their eye as they walk by, even if it exists only in memory.

## MARKET SQUARE FARMERS' MARKET, 301 KING STREET

Venture to City Hall any Saturday morning, year-round, and you'll find a bustle of activity taking place in Market Square, the plaza in front of the city's seat of government. Farmers hawk in-season vegetables, ranging from the well-known—tomatoes, potatoes, onions, kale—to the specifically seasonal—ramps, carnival squash and more. Other vendors come out, too, selling homemade jam, hand-illustrated notecards, seasonal wreaths and hand-sewn children's clothing.

> *The Farmers' Market in the heart of Alexandria at Market Square is believed to be the oldest farmers' market in continuing operation in the United States.*
>
> *It can be admired and examined from many standpoints. From the shoppers' point of view, the Market is a wonderful place to buy fresh produce, flowers, and things for the home and kitchen. It's also a unique opportunity to chat with friends and neighbors who share their enthusiasm for the Market. Regular shoppers at the Farmers' Market have also formed friendships with the vendors from whom they have been purchasing goods for years, even decades.*[128]

In true Alexandria fashion, the city's farmers' market has been in existence since the mid-1700s and has operated since, making it one of the country's oldest continuously running markets.

The farmers' market on the front porch of City Hall has survived and thrived for nearly three centuries. *Hope Nelson.*

Market Square was founded 1749 by an act of the House of Burgesses.

*Originally, Market Square was little more than a scruffy field where housewares, foodstuffs, animals and farm products could be sold to local townspeople or those coming to Alexandria from its rural hinterlands. The area was also used for other purposes, such as the sale of African slaves and the mustering of militias. By the late 18th century, the square started to fill with permanent structures and buildings providing a home for prospering commercial sellers, taverns and warehouses.*[129]

Quickly, the market became a community gathering place, inviting dozens of neighbors to come back week after week, essentially raising whole generations of families with market visits and traditions.

*Mrs. (Louisa) Reinhardt made her first trip to the market in 1911, shortly after her husband died, when she had an 18-acre chicken farm on Edsall Road in Fairfax County.*

Now in the shadow of City Hall, the farmers' market bounced around a bit during the 1900s but has come to a familiar home at Alexandria's Market Square. *Hope Nelson.*

*"The market was quite a place then," she recalled during a [1971] interview. "Everybody had a covered stall. They slaughtered pigs and chickens right in the square."*

*"I always brought my chickens dressed, though. We got 35 cents a pound then; it's way up to 50 cents now."*[130]

The farmers' market remained largely untouched by city business until the government's plans for "urban renewal" began to take shape in the mid-1900s. By 1960, the market was threatened with an uncertain future; as plans for a renewed City Hall and surrounding plaza began to take shape, the familiar farmers' market found itself marginalized to side streets, much to the consternation of both vendors and customers.

*Workmen began tearing down Alexandria's historic farmers' market this morning preparatory to construction work on the four-story south wing of City Hall along Market Alley.*

*The sheds, which have protected farmers and their Saturday morning patrons and formed a picturesque touch to the alley, once known as Sharpshin Alley, gave the first tangible evidence that the construction work will start within a few days.*

*Next Saturday the farmers who can be accommodated will set up stalls in the abandoned surplus store shop the second door south of Market Alley on N. Royal Street. It is owned by the city.*[131]

Thus, in 1960, the market moved to 113 North Royal Street, adjacent to the new City Hall development. It moved again, to the 300 block of Cameron Street, while construction persisted for nearly a decade. At times, the future of the market looked bleak, especially after its move to Cameron Street; many farmers and customers weren't sure the tradition would survive the decade of upheaval. But it did.

By the 1970s, the farmers' market had once again settled back into the renewed Market Square, spreading out and expanding to fill the plaza fully over the years. "Saturday morning market is the busiest time of the week for the Market Square, and this morning, the incoming of the meats, poultry and showy vegetables and April fruits offered an ample assortment for tomorrow's dinner; so crowds have gathered there on Saturdays ever since Alexandria became a town."[132]

Nearly three centuries after the farmers' market made its debut on Alexandria's landscape, it's thriving as well as ever. From the sunniest summer Saturdays to the snowiest winter mornings, its pull brings in hundreds of customers each week. Though styles and food tastes have changed, the market has remained a vibrant part of the community's fabric.

## BILBO BAGGINS, 208 QUEEN STREET

At first glance, Queen Street in Old Town seems a strange place to put a *Hobbit*-themed restaurant. This isn't Middle Earth, after all. But after a few minutes sitting inside Bilbo Baggins—either in the pub or the restaurant proper—it all begins to make sense. The coziness of the establishment practically exudes through the walls, eschewing formality for the sake of friendliness.

Bilbo Baggins launched in 1980, when Old Town Alexandria was quite different than it is today. But the historic, quaint nature of Alexandria architecture piqued the interest of owner and chef Michael Armellino, and he set down roots on a quiet block a couple of streets off of King.

While some things have changed over the years, this review from 1982 discussing the hominess of the restaurant still rings true, in all the best ways:

> *The small dining rooms, one upstairs and one down, have a pleasant, chunky, hobbit-like roughness, with wood floors and tables, old brick and varnished lathing strips in the walls, and, in the center of the downstairs room, a brick oven for baking bread. Downstairs are a series of high French doors, open to the street when the weather's right. A streetside table can offer the pleasures of a sidewalk café minus the flies and sparrows, and on a cool evening when there's a soft river breeze, the sitting is a delight.*[133]

The food itself has always been inventive and often ahead of its time, with consideration of vegetarian cuisine and other special dietary needs before many restaurants did, for instance. Even in the early 1990s, its menu offered options for many palates.

> *The low-cholesterol, low-sodium, low-calorie and vegetarian dishes go beyond the obvious: A variation on salad nicoise is topped with grilled lemon shrimp or poached salmon. There is a grilled chicken salad with grilled vegetables, and a salad of apples, oranges, walnuts and feta with dill*

Bilbo Baggins Restaurant is a quirky little café on Queen Street, several blocks away from the hubbub of Old Town's main drag. *Hope Nelson.*

Bilbo Baggins launched in 1980, when Old Town Alexandria was quite different than it is today. *Hope Nelson.*

*in a walnut-raspberry vinaigrette....Aimed at vegetarians, but universally appealing, is the tortilla pizza, which is listed as an appetizer but is large enough to be an entrée or an appetizer for two. It is paper-thin, plate-size crisp dough weighted with slices of fresh tomato and roasted pepper and dotted with melted mozzarella and gratings of Parmesan, plus black olives and herbs, with a faint tang of balsamic vinegar.*[134]

Now nearly forty years old, Bilbo Baggins is still as fresh as a daisy. Every night, there's a motley gathering of friends (and strangers who become friends) in the Green Dragon Pub adjacent to the dining room, and the kitchen wheels and deals friendly fare to hungry diners in the restaurant proper. It's a long way from Middle Earth, but just as cozy.

# THE CURSE OF 100 KING STREET

It's no secret that the restaurant business is a tough one. Nearly half of all eateries fail at some point or another, so it's not a surprise that Alexandria has seen considerable turnover from year to year. But one location has seen more dramatics and theatrics than many—the building at 100 King Street, just a half block from the Potomac River.

As with many structures in Old Town, the land that played host to 100 King has a connection to the Washingtons. "Lot 51, at the corner of King and Water/Lee streets was originally purchased in 1749 by Lawrence Washington, George Washington's half brother, and the lot would eventually pass to John Fitzgerald and Valentine Peers, who banked out the land into the Potomac."[135]

Despite the laundry list of restaurants it's known over the years, the actual building that sits at 100 King hasn't changed much in more than a century, at least regarding its façade. Beginning its history as the Corn Exchange in 1871, the grand structure played host to a grocery store on the first floor and the Corn Exchange on the second.[136]

> *The Corn Exchange itself did not last long, but Lindsey's grocery business fared much better. By 1922 the* Alexandria Gazette *had the following to say about what had become of the Lindsey-Nicholson Corporation:*
>
> *"No firm has been more responsible for the development of Alexandria commercially, and with some 4000 square ft. of floor space in its large brick building at 100–110 King Street, it is the center of the wholesale district. It handles a complete line of staple and fancy groceries, notions, flour, feedstuff, etc. as well as the celebrated Diamond tires and tubes."*[137]

The building moved away from food sales by the 1920s and became the Virginia Public Service Company. At midcentury, it fell into the hands of the federal government. Only after that period did it begin its second career as a food purveyor, with each owner or lessee more interesting than the previous one.

First, the longtime Italian restaurant owners the Landini brothers (featured in chapter one) took up residence in 1976, opening a restaurant by the name of Pellicano. A precursor to their eponymous establishment a little farther up King Street, the restaurant had three years of service before closing.[138] The Heidleburg Restaurant moved in to hawk German food in the

The building at 100 King Street, shown here in June 1985, began its life as the Corn Exchange. *Alexandria Library Local History Special Collections.*

1980s, and by 1990, the owners of the Fish Market across the street opened two different eateries in the space—the Gaslight and, more popularly, the Alamo, a southwestern-themed restaurant that had nearly a decade of life. The Alamo closed in 2000, a victim of rising rents.[139]

At the dawn of the new millennium, the 100 King building sat vacant for nearly six years, after which time the appropriately named small-plates purveyor 100 King opened its doors. It shuttered again two years later, in 2008, and two years after that, an Asian restaurant, Red Curry, tried its hand at the space. An attempt to build on the space of their other restaurant holding, Mai Thai on The Strand, the business owners couldn't find traction and closed in 2012.[140]

A new era dawned when international Italian-food magnate Antonio Carluccio prepared to open his newest outpost—the first Carluccio's to open in the United States—at 100 King in 2015. The big name and weighty restaurant history seemed to indicate that the curse was over.

"They opened Carluccio's and even the big owner from Europe came," said Jay Roberts, the writer behind Old Town blog *Jaybird's Jottings*, who went to the restaurant on opening day. "It was like, 'This is it—the curse is over.'"[141]

*Above*: Over its long life, the building at 100 King Street has played host to many restaurants, many of which have failed in very short order, lending speculation to a possible curse. *Hope Nelson*.

*Left*: For a time, 100 King played host to the Bavarian Room, pictured here in 1985. *Alexandria Library Local History Special Collections*.

But two years later, news spread through town that Carluccio's had closed its doors unexpectedly, leaving even waitstaff in the lurch. Calls to the corporate office went unanswered; the Bethesda, Maryland location also shuttered, essentially ending Carluccio's American presence in one fell swoop. Thus, 100 King found itself adrift yet again, looking for a renter or a buyer, sitting vacant all the while on one of Old Town's most iconic corners, in one of its most recognizable buildings.

The year 2018 saw the dawn of yet another restaurant concept to move in; a concept that remains open and thriving at press time. And the corporate executive chef of Mia's, the new Italian and pizza eatery from Alexandria Restaurant Partners, has downplayed any thought of a so-called curse.

> *"I keep hearing about it's a cursed space, but it's the best corner in Old Town,"* [Graham] *Duncan exclaimed. "I think all you have to do is put a good restaurant here and it'll fly. That's really the only thing that's missing is a good restaurant.... Carluccio's to me was very European, and I don't think it translated well."* [142]

While the two-year clock is ticking for Mia's, all signs point to success for the restaurant at the moment. But the idea of a decades-old curse is hard to move away from. Has the curse been broken? Time will tell.

# Notes

## Chapter One

1. Kabler, *Story of Gadsby's Tavern*, 20.
2. O'Brien, *Virginia's Historic Restaurants*, 122.
3. *Alexandria Gazette*, "Gadsby's to Open on Feb. 16."
4. Ibid.
5. Feller, "Gadsby's Recreates Tradition."
6. *Washington Post*, "Don't Leave Gadsby's Tavern to the Tourists."
7. Shuman's Bakery, "An Alexandria Tradition."
8. Mansfield, "Good Old Boys at Shuman's."
9. Sullivan, "Revived from Century-Old Bakery."
10. Harvey and Stansfield, "Shuman's Bakery," *Pictorial History of Alexandria*, 104.
11. Sullivan, "Revived from Century-Old Bakery."
12. Nelson, "Shuman's Jelly Cake Serves Up Generations of Memories."
13. Williams, "Robert Portner and Alexandria's Pre-Prohibition Brewing History."
14. Ibid.
15. "Portner's Brewhouse Reopening this Week," *Alexandria Gazette Packet*, March 9, 2017.
16. "Drunk History: Visiting the Storied Portner Brewhouse in Alexandria, Va." *Conde Nast Traveler*, January 18, 2017, https://www.cntraveler.com.
17. "Portner's Brewhouse Reopening this Week," *Alexandria Gazette Packet*.

18. "After 100 Years, Royal's Family Is Still Cooking," *Washington Post*.
19. "Charlie Euripides: Giving Back to His Adopted Country," *Alexandria Gazette Packet*.
20. "After 100 Years, Royal's Family Is Still Cooking."
21. Dresden, "Mount Vernon Inn."
22. Hodge, "Family Out."
23. Sugarman, "Mount Vernon Inn."
24. Landini Brothers review, *Washington Post*, September 15, 1983.
25. Robb Report, "Where There's Smoke."
26. "Tiffany Tavern Stands Alone," *Washington Post*.
27. Ibid.

*Chapter Two*

28. Riker, "Chadwicks on the Strand."
29. Ibid.
30. Ibid.
31. Ibid.
32. Epitropoulos, "Chadwicks Celebrates 50 Years."
33. Evans, "Chili Chain with a Choice Recipe."
34. Rothschild and Zwerdling, "Hard Times Café."
35. McKenna, "Hard Times Café."
36. Richman, "Southern Accents."
37. Ibid.
38. Richman, "Union Street's Great Public Service."
39. Ibid.
40. Richman, "Generous George."
41. "Secrets of Longevity."
42. Ibid.
43. Ibid.
44. Ibid.
45. Solomon, "Happy Meals."
46. Ruhe, "People at Work."
47. Salmon, "Balancing Old School Meals."
48. Ibid.
49. Dodds, "Mad Men."
50. Porter, "Hamburger Chains Vie for Area Trade."
51. *Washington Post*, "F.T. Callahan, Ex-Navy Officer."

52. *Alexandria Gazette Packet*, "Friends in Heat Are Friends in Sweets."
53. Alcala, "Go on an Ice Cream–Fueled Crawl."
54. Epitropoulos, "Alexandria Restaurant Partners."
55. Attner, "Joe Theismann, Incorporated."
56. Epitropoulos, "Alexandria Restaurant Partners."
57. *Washington Post*, "Dream On, Del Ray."
58. Nelson, "Dairy Godmother Says Goodbye."
59. Kelly, "A Fairy Tale Come True."
60. Ibid.


*Chapter Three*

61. Riker, "Fitzgerald's Warehouse, King and Union Streets."
62. Ibid.
63. Ibid.
64. Ibid.
65. Mulvihill and McGrath, "Green Party in Alexandria."
66. Richman, "Sorting It Out at the Warehouse."
67. *Alexandria Gazette*, September 28, 1866.
68. Ibid., May 10, 1909.
69. Richman, *Washington Post*.
70. Ruhe, "Meet the Chef."
71. "Cedar Knoll," Alexandria Visitor Center.
72. Feller, "Family Out."
73. Ibid.
74. Richman, "Fall Dining: Country Inns."
75. Peterson, "Mount Vernon."
76. Ibid.
77. Office of Historic Alexandria, "Out of the Attic."
78. Ibid.
79. Riker, "0 Prince Street."
80. *Alexandria Times*, "Cash Grocer Packs Up."
81. Ibid.
82. Applar, "Historic Buildings and Places on the Waterfront."
83. Barnett and Barnett, "RT's Restaurant."
84. Richman, "My 50 Favorites."
85. Gilbertson, "Creole and Cajun?"
86. Ibid.

87. Ibid.
88. Ibid.
89. Ibid.
90. Interview with Fish Market general manager Jesse Mass, April 3, 2019.
91. Dresden, "Fish Market, Ruffino's."
92. Mass interview.
93. Tagert, "Fish Market Restaurant."
94. "Our Story," the Wharf, http://wharfrestaurant.com.
95. Ibid.
96. Dresden, "The Wharf: Nets, Pulleys and Fresh Fish," *Washington Post*.
97. McKenna, "The Wharf: This Club Plays with a Full Deck," *Washington Post*.
98. Landers, "Hot Time in the Old Town as River Rises," *Washington Post*.

### Chapter Four

99. Richman, "Friendly Fare at Trattoria da Franco."
100. Ibid.
101. Nelson, "Old Trattoria Is New Again."
102. Richman, "Two Newcomers to Old Town."
103. Richman, "Le Gaulois."
104. Stieglitz, "At Le Gaulois, Pike Peaks."
105. Marchetti, "Dishes of India Beckons."
106. Ibid.
107. Ibid.
108. Carman, "$20 Diner."
109. Sietsema, "Taqueria Poblano."
110. Ibid.
111. Carman, "$20 Diner."
112. Marchetti, "Alexandria's Chez Andree."
113. "Stanley Lecureux: Owner of Chez Andree."
114. Marchetti, "Alexandria's Chez Andree."

### Chapter Five

115. Somers, "Stories Pour from Virginia Pub Owner."
116. Radcliffe, "O'Reagan's Pub Lunch."

117. MacDonnell, "Ireland's Own to Relocate."

118. Callahan, "Ireland's Own Files for Bankruptcy."

119. Schrott, "Pat Troy, Alexandria St. Patrick's Day Parade Founder."

120. *Alexandria Gazette Packet*, "Not Your Average Cup of Joe."

121. Ross, "Escape the Grind at Misha's."

122. Ibid.

123. *Alexandria Times*, "Cash Grocer Packs Up."

124. *Alexandria Gazette Packet*, "Cash Grocer Cashes Out."

125. Ibid.

126. Ibid.

127. Ibid.

128. Hynan, "A Saturday Morning Ritual."

129. Office of Historic Alexandria, "Evolution of Market Square."

130. Edwards, "Market's Friends Loyal."

131. *Alexandria Gazette*, "Farmers' Market Being Razed Today."

132. *Alexandria Gazette*, "News of Long Ago: 1898."

133. Barnett and Barnett, "Bilbo Baggins."

134. Richman, "Bilbo Woos and Wows."

135. Applar, "Historic Buildings and Places on the Waterfront."

136. Ibid.

137. Ibid.

138. Epitropoulos, "What's Behind the Curse of 100 King?"

139. Ibid.

140. Ibid.

141. Ibid.

142. Nelson, "Mia's Adds American-Italian Flair."

# Bibliography

Alcala, Brianne. "Go on an Ice Cream–Fueled Crawl of Old Town Alexandria," *Washington Post*, July 23, 2015.

*Alexandria Gazette*. September 28, 1866.

———. May 10, 1909.

———. "Farmers' Market Being Razed Today." July 5, 1960.

———. "Gadsby's To Open on Feb. 16." January 12, 1976.

———. "News of Long Ago: 1898." July 27, 1942.

*Alexandria Gazette Packet*. "Cash Grocer Cashes Out." August 14, 2007.

———. "Charlie Euripides: Giving Back to His Adopted Country," July 18, 2018.

———. "Friends in Heat Are Friends in Sweets." August 20, 2003

———. "Not Your Average Cup of Joe." August 5, 2008.

———. "Portner's Brewhouse Reopening this Week." March 9, 2017.

———. "Secrets of Longevity." February 25, 2002.

*Alexandria Times*. "Cash Grocer Packs Up." August 23, 2007.

Alexandria Visitor Center, "Cedar Knoll." https://www.visitalexandriava.com.

Applar, Douglas. "Historic Buildings and Places on the Waterfront." City of Alexandria, 2008.

Attner, Paul. "Joe Theismann, Incorporated." *Washington Post*, August 31, 1980.

Barnett, Mark, and Gail Barnett. "Bilbo Baggins." *Washington Post Magazine*, August 15, 1982.

————. "RT's Restaurant." *Washington Post Magazine.* August 17, 1986.

Brace, Eric. "Tiffany Tavern Stands Alone." *Washington Post*, April 20, 2001.

Callahan, Katie. "Ireland's Own Files for Bankruptcy." *Alexandria Times*, June 20, 2014.

Carman, Tim. "The $20 Diner: Taqueria Poblano Offers Mexican Cuisine by Way of California." *Washington Post*, August 22, 2013.

Chadwicks Restaurant. "A Brief History of 203 South Strand, Alexandria, Virginia."

Dodds, Eric. "Mad Men: A Brief History of the Real-World Burger Chef." *Time*, May 19, 2004.

Dresden, Donald. "Fish Market, Ruffino's: Something Fishy or Italian." *Washington Post*, November 14, 1976.

————. "Mount Vernon Inn." *Washington Post*, August 18, 1974.

————. "The Wharf: Nets, Pulleys and Fresh Fish." *Washington Post*, September 28, 1975.

Edwards, Paul G. "Market's Friends Loyal." *Washington Post*, September 9, 1971.

Epitropoulos, Alexa. "Alexandria Restaurant Partners Buy Equity Interest in Theismann's Restaurant." *Alexandria Times*, February 9, 2018.

————. "Chadwicks Celebrates 50 Years." *Alexandria Times*, November 22, 2017.

————. "What's Behind the Curse of 100 King?" *Alexandria Times*, July 6, 2017.

Evans, Judith. "The Chili Chain with a Choice Recipe for Expansion." *Washington Post*, March 24, 1997.

Feller, Susan. "Family Out." *Washington Post*, April 10, 1980.

————. "Gadsby's Recreates Tradition." *Washington Journal*, March 4, 1976.

Gilbertson, Kris. "Creole and Cajun? RT's Is the Place to Be!" *Zebra Press*, March 2018.

Harvey, Karen G., and Ross Stansfield. *A Pictoral History of Alexandria.* Virginia Beach, VA: Donning Company, 1977.

Hodge, Paul. "Family Out." *Washington Post*, September 1, 1977.

Hynan, John. "A Saturday Morning Ritual." *Alexandria Gazette Packet*, May 7, 1988.

Kabler, Dorothy H. *The Story of Gadsby's Tavern.* Alexandria, VA: Newell-Cole Company, 1952.

Kelly, John. "A Fairy Tale Come True: The Dairy Godmother Has a New Owner." *Washington Post*, June 13, 2017.

Landers, Jim. "Hot Time in the Old Town as River Rises." *Washington Post*, June 24, 1972.

MacDonnell, Clare. "Ireland's Own to Relocate, Change Name to Pat Troy's." *Arlington Catholic Herald*, July 30, 1999.

Mansfield, Stephanie. "The Good Old Boys at Shuman's." *Washington Post*, August 12, 1978.

Marchetti, Domenica. "After 100 Years, Royal's Family Is Still Cooking." *Washington Post*, June 24, 2004.

———. "Alexandria's Chez Andrée Sticks to the Basics with Classic French Dishes." *Washington Post*, January 31, 2002.

———. "Dishes of India Beckons with Flavorful Fare, Service." *Washington Post*, April 5, 2001.

Marcus, Lilit. "Drunk History: Visiting the Storied Portner Brewhouse in Alexandria, Va." *Conde Nast Traveler*, January 18, 2017.

Mass, Jesse. Interview with Hope Nelson. April 3, 2019.

McKenna, Barbara. "Hard Times Café: Grand Chili and a Great Jukebox to Boot." *Washington Post*, April 13, 1984.

———. "The Wharf: This Club Plays with a Full Deck." *Washington Post*, April 6, 1984.

Mulvihill, Grace, and Anne McGrath. "Green Party in Alexandria." *Washington Post*, March 9, 1990.

Nelson, Hope. "Dairy Godmother Says Goodbye to Del Ray." *Alexandria Gazette Packet*, January 18, 2017.

———. "Mia's Adds American-Italian Flair to King Street." *Alexandria Gazette Packet*, May 18, 2018.

———. "Old Trattoria Is New Again in Alexandria." *Alexandria Gazette-Packet*, March 18, 2018.

———. "Portner's Brewhouse Reopening This Week." *Alexandria Gazette Packet*, March 9, 2017.

———. "Shuman's Jelly Cake Serves Up Generations of Memories." EdibleDC. http://edibledc.com.

O'Brien, Dawn. *Virginia's Historic Restaurants and Their Recipes*. Durham, NC: Blair, 1989.

Office of Historic Alexandria. "The Evolution of Market Square." *Alexandria Times*, August 14, 2014.

———. "Out of the Attic: Beachcombers Restaurant." *Alexandria Times*, September 17–23, 2009.

Peterson, Tim. "Mount Vernon: Inside Cedar Knoll." *Mount Vernon Gazette*, October 20, 2016.

Porter, Frank C. "Hamburger Chains Vie for Area Trade." *Washington Post*, July 14, 1959.

Radcliffe, Donnie. "O'Reagan's Pub Lunch." *Washington Post*, March 18, 1988.

Richman, Phyllis. "Bilbo Woos and Wows." *Washington Post*, December 20, 1992.

———. "Fall Dining: Country Inns." *Washington Post Magazine*, October 16, 1977.

———. "Friendly Fare at Trattoria da Franco." *Washington Post*, March 15, 1987.

———. "Generous George." *Washington Post Dining Guide*, November 1996.

———. "Le Gaulois." *Washington Post*, November 1996.

———. "My 50 Favorites." *Washington Post*, September 20, 1987.

———. "Sorting It Out at the Warehouse." *Washington Post*, July 10, 1988.

———. "Southern Accents." *Washington Post*, February 13, 1994.

———. "Two Newcomers to Old Town." *Washington Post*, June 12, 1988.

———. "Union Street's Great Public Service." *Washington Post Magazine*, April 5, 1987.

Riker, Diane. "Chadwicks on the Strand." City of Alexandria, 2009.

———. "Fitzgerald's Warehouse, King and Union Streets." City of Alexandria, 2008.

———. "0 Prince Street: A Timeline." City of Alexandria, 2008.

The Robb Report. "Where There's Smoke." April 1, 2012. https://robbreport.com/food-drink/spirits/where-theres-smoke-233816/

Ross, Kelly Mae. "Escape the Grind at Misha's Casual, Artsy Coffeehouse." *The Hill*, July 6, 2011.

Rothschild, Barbara, and Daniel Zwerdling. "Hard Times Café." *Washington Post*, August 11, 1983.

———. "Landini Brothers 115 King St., Alexandria." *Washington Post*, September 15, 1983.

Ruhe, Shirley. "Meet the Chef: Sert Ruamthong of Warehouse." *Mount Vernon Gazette*. July 14–20, 2016.

———. "People at Work: Sharing Food and Conversation." *Alexandria Gazette Packet*, November 1, 2016.

Salmon, Mike. "Balancing Old School Meals with New School Marketing in Alexandria." *Alexandria Gazette Packet*, April 30, 2018.

Schrott, Missy. "Pat Troy, Alexandria St. Patrick's Day Parade Founder, Dies at 76." *Alexandria Times*, March 22, 2018.

Shuman's Bakery. "An Alexandria, Virginia Tradition." https://www.shumansbakery.com.

Sietsema, Tom. "Taqueria Poblano, Home of the Baby Taco." *Washington Post*, December 15, 1999.

Solomon, Mary Jane. "Happy Meals." *Washington Post*, September 9, 1994.

Somers, Meredith. "Stories Pour from Virginia Pub Owner at Ireland's Own." *Washington Times*, December 25, 2011.

Stieglitz, Peggy. "At Le Gaulois, Pike Peaks." *Washington Post*, July 10, 1988.

Sugarman, Carole. "Mount Vernon Inn." *Washington Post Magazine*, July 7, 1985.

Sullivan, Patricia. "Revived from Century-Old Bakery, Shuman's Jelly Cake Is Alexandria's Madeleine." *Washington Post*, December 15, 2011.

Tagert, Bob. "Fish Market Restaurant and Anchor Bar." *Old Town Crier*, November 25, 2016.

Theismann, Jeanne. "Charlie Euripides: Giving Back to His Adopted Country." *Alexandria Gazette Packet*, July 18, 2018.

*Washington Post*. "After 100 Years, Royal's Family Is Still Cooking." June 24, 2004,

———. "Don't Leave Gadsby's Tavern to the Tourists." November 9, 1984.

———. "Dream On, Del Ray," June 5, 2002.

———. "F.T. Callahan, Ex-Navy Officer, Ran Burger Chef." January 3, 1979.

———. "Stanley Lecureux; Owner of Chez Andrée in Alexandria." November 23, 2005.

Williams, Mike. "Robert Portner and Alexandria's Pre-Prohibition Brewing History." *Boundary Stones*, January 27, 2016. https://blogs.weta.org/boundarystones/2016/01/27/robert-portner-and-alexandrias-pre-prohibition-brewing-history.

# Index

# T

# U

# W

# About the Author

By day, Hope Nelson is a marketing manager at The Motley Fool. By night, weekends and holidays, she's a food writer and restaurant columnist always on the lookout for the next tasty meal. Hope is the "Appetite" columnist for the *Alexandria Gazette Packet* and has written for *VegNews* magazine and *EdibleDC*. A native of Tallahassee, Florida, she has a master's degree in American and Florida studies from Florida State University and is an obsessive fan of all Seminole sports. In her free time, she volunteers at the Animal Welfare League of Alexandria and races in long-distance triathlons and marathons. She and her husband live in Old Town Alexandria.

*Visit us at*
www.historypress.com